MW01474474

PRECIOUS MOMENTS™

DAILY BREAD FOR GIRLS AND BOYS

Walking with God

Art by Sam Butcher

Copyright © 1997
Child Evangelism Fellowship® Inc.

All artwork is copyrighted and cannot be reproduced
in any form without written permission from
PRECIOUS MOMENTS, INC.
No portion of the text may be reproduced
without permission of the publisher.

Contents

God, You Are Enough .... Ruth P. Overholtzer

Did You Know Jesus Is Called the Lovely One? .... Ruth P. Overholtzer

Lord Jesus, Teach Us How to Pray .... Ruth P. Overholtzer

I Think the Holy Spirit Must Be Like a Dove .... Ruth P. Overholtzer

Jesus Died for You and Me .... Doris Seger

God's Word Is Really Powerful! .... Elsie Lippy, coordinator

Don't Be Sad, God Cares .... Vera Hutchcroft

Maranatha .... V. Leona Cross

Be Attitudes .... Elsie Lippy

It's Sure Hard to Believe You're a Christian .... Elsie Lippy

We're Finding What God Wants Us to Do .... Joyce Worrall

Do You Love Jesus? .... Hope Irvin Marston

God, You Are Enough

Day 1   Read Genesis 1:1

Hide and Seek Words ☐
As you read your Bible try to find these hidden words:

"In the beginning God"

God Did It!

How did this wonderful world in which we live come to be? God Almighty, the great Creator, made the heavens and the earth. Many people who think they are wise have tried to figure out other ways that the world could have been made. But I would rather believe God, wouldn't you? The Bible tells us that He made the world out of nothing and that He hung it on nothing! Who but God Almighty could do that?

> I believe in God the Father,
> Who made us ev'ry one,
> Who made the earth and heaven,
> The moon and stars and sun;
> All that we have each day,
> To us by Him is giv'n;
> We call Him when we pray,
> "Our Father God in heav'n."
>
>   Annie E. Hall

Day 2　　　　　　　　　Read John 4:23, 24

Hide and Seek Words ☐

As you read your Bible try to find hidden words:

"God is a Spirit"

What God Is Like

God is a Spirit. That means, for one thing, that we cannot see God. We read in John 1:18, "No man hath seen God at any time...."

When the Lord Jesus, God's Son, came to earth, He came to show us what God is like. Jesus said, "...he that hath seen me hath seen the Father." All the wonder, the beauty, the goodness, and love that were in the Lord Jesus show us what God is like.

What do you know about the Lord Jesus that shows you what God is like?

_____

_____

_____

_____

Day 3   Read Matthew 28:19, 20

Hide and Seek Words ☐

As you read your Bible try to find these hidden words:

"...the Father...the Son, and...the Holy Ghost [Spirit]"

Three in One

I believe God's Holy Spirit
Lives in my heart today,
And though I've often grieved Him,
He never goes away.
The Father, Son and Spirit
Are the great One in Three;
We worship and adore Him,
The blessed Trinity.

                    Annie E. Hall

God is one person and yet He is three persons—Father, Son, and Spirit. Three in one is called a Trinity. We will never understand all about the Trinity until we get to Heaven. But we do know that God the Heavenly *Father* sent His *Son* the Lord Jesus to this earth to die for our sins, and the *Holy Spirit* comes to live in our hearts when we believe on the Lord Jesus as our Savior from sin.

Day 4   Read Psalm 90:1, 2

Hide and Seek Words ☐

As you read your Bible try to find these hidden words:

"... from everlasting to everlasting, thou art God"

God Never Changes

God had no beginning and will have no ending. He always was, He always is, and He always shall be! We believe this because the Bible tells us so.

Another thing about God is that He does not change. He said, "For I am the Lord, I change not..." (Malachi 3:6). We are very changeable and so are our friends. One day they are very friendly with us, but the next day they may have found someone else whom they would rather play with. So they leave us alone. How wonderful it is to know that God never changes! His love for us is always the same.

Day 5   Read Isaiah 6:3

Hide and Seek Words ☐

As you read your Bible try to find these hidden words:

"Holy, holy, holy, is the Lord"

God Is Holy

Did you know that you have never seen your own face? When you look in the mirror you do not see your face, but an image of it. We have already learned that no one has seen God.

In the Bible we read about a man by the name of Isaiah. Isaiah saw God "sitting upon a throne, high and lifted up...." Angels around the throne covered their faces and cried, "Holy, holy, holy, is the Lord." When Isaiah saw God's holiness, he could only cry out that he was a sinner and not fit to stand before God.

God is holy. This means He has no sin. But we have all sinned. We cannot live with God because of our sin. When Jesus died on the cross, He took *our sin* so we may be forgiven.

Day 6　　　　　　　　　　　　Read 2 Corinthians 5:21

Hide and Seek Words ☐

As you read your Bible try to find these hidden words:

"... he [God] hath made him [Jesus] to be sin for us"

Punished for Me

"When did you become a Christian?" a minister once asked a boy. "The day the bee stung Mother," he replied. The minister thought that was strange so he asked him to explain.

"Well," said the boy, "I could not understand how Jesus' dying could save me. One day while on the porch a bee flew around me. I was afraid of bees and was sure he would sting me. I called Mother and she came out. When she saw the bee was about to sting me, she put her hand between my hand and the bee. The bee stung Mother and did not sting me.

"*Then* I understood what the Lord Jesus had done for me. He had taken the punishment for sin in my place. What Mother had often tried to explain, I understood at last. I then believed on Jesus as my own Savior."

Day 7   Read John 3:16

Hide and Seek Words ☐

As you read your Bible try to find these hidden words:

"God . . . gave his only begotten Son"

Forgotten?

One time a little child said, "For God so loved the world that he gave his only *forgotten* Son...." instead of "begotten Son." A minister asked her, "Do you know *why* God 'forgot' His Son? It was because the Lord wanted to remember *you*. God in Heaven was willing to part with His Son for a little while that He might have you for ever.... He let Him die so that He could give you everlasting life. It was for you that God 'forgot' His Son."*

So dear—so very dear to God
More dear I cannot be;
The love wherewith He loves the Son,
Such is His love for me.

*Walter Wilson

Day 8   Read 2 Timothy 2:19

Hide and Seek Words ☐
As you read your Bible try to find these hidden words:
"The Lord knoweth them that are his"

God Knows

Did you ever try to count the stars? How many do you suppose there are? We could never count them all. But God not only knows their number; He has them all named and calls them by their names (Psalm 147:4)!

Try counting the hairs on your head! Now I hear you laughing and saying, "I cannot do that!" But God knows the number of hairs on your head (Matthew 10:30).

God knows everything. He knows that all of us have sinned and need a Savior. He knows those who are His. "His" are all who have believed the Lord Jesus died for their sin and *received* Him. If you have not received Him, will you do so just now? After you have truly done this, you may sign your name in the space below.

name _____

date _____

Day 9   Read 1 John 4:7-10

Hide and Seek Words ☐

As you read your Bible try to find these hidden words:

"God is love"

God Loves

Can you tell what the word "love" means? It is a longing for and a delight in someone. Think of God's love.

1. God loves His Son (Matthew 3:17).
2. God loves the world—every person in it (John 3:16).
3. God loves His enemies—sinners (Ephesians 2:4, 5).
4. God loves in a very special way those who love His Son (John 16:27).

Sometimes after you have done wrong, you think that God does not love you anymore. But He does, and He wants you to talk to Him in prayer. He will forgive you when you tell Him about your sin.

I am so glad that our Father in heaven,
Tells of His love in the book He has given;
Wonderful things in the Bible I see,
This is the dearest, that Jesus loves me.
                        —P. P. Bliss

Day 10   Read Psalm 145:17-19

Hide and Seek Words ☐

As you read your Bible try to find these hidden words:

"The Lord is righteous in all his ways"

God Is Right

Many years ago a teacher made a rule that any child who told a lie be punished with six strokes on the hand. Soon a little girl told a lie. She was so tiny that the teacher hated to punish her; but he had to if there was to be order in the school. She cried so hard after the first stroke that he felt he could not go on. He looked over to the boys and asked, "Is there anyone who is willing to take her punishment?" One boy bravely stepped up and took the punishment which belonged to the girl.

God is love but He always does what is right. He must punish sin. He cannot just overlook it. You and I deserve punishment because we are sinners. The Lord Jesus willingly took our punishment when He died on the cross.

God said it,
Jesus did it;
I believe it;
That settles it.

Day 11   Read Romans 5:8, 9

Hide and Seek Words ☐
As you read your Bible try to find these hidden words:

"... while we were yet sinners"

God Cared

A young man, who had done many sinful things, once went to visit his pastor. He told him about many of his sins, and after each one of them he would say, "But I don't care about that!"

The pastor said to the young fellow, "Will you promise me to do one thing?" The boy promised, so the pastor said, "Every night for one week bow your head and say, 'O Jesus Christ, You have died for my sin, but I don't care about that.'" That night the young man tried to say it, but he couldn't finish the last part. On the fourth night he went to the pastor and told him, "I could not say it. How could I not care when Jesus suffered so much for my sins? I want to follow Him!"

You do care that Jesus died for you, I know. Have you thanked Him for taking your punishment for sin?

Day 12 Read 1 John 1:8, 9

Hide and Seek Words ☐

As you read your Bible try to find these hidden words:

"If we confess our sins, he is faithful and just to forgive us our sins"

God Forgives

What happens when we sin after we have invited the Lord Jesus to come into our hearts? Does God still love us? Oh, yes, He does; but that sin makes Him sad. Just as soon as you know you have done wrong, ask His forgiveness, no matter where you are.

You know how it is when you have done something that displeases your father and mother. There isn't a very happy feeling between you and them. But when you say you are sorry and ask for forgiveness, everything is made right again. That is the way it is with God and you. You need to talk to Him in prayer when you have sinned.

When God forgives, He forgets,
When God forgives, He forgets;
No more He remembers our sins,
When God forgives, He forgets.
—Robert Harkness

Day 13   Read Ephesians 4:30-32

Hide and Seek Words ☐

As you read your Bible try to find these hidden words:

". . . forgiving one another"

You Forgive

"What! Going out to play with *him* again? I thought you quarreled only last evening and were never going to play with each other again. Funny memory you have!" said Jimmy's older sister. But Jimmy flashed a satisfied smile. "Roland and I are good forgetters," he said.

It's a good idea to be a forgetter when someone has done wrong to you. Because the Lord Jesus Christ died in your place, God can forgive and forget your sins. He tells you that since He has forgiven you, you ought to forgive others. If you will remember how much God has forgiven you, you will not find it hard to do.

> Help us to do the things we should,
> To be to others kind and good;
> In all we do in work or play,
> To love You better day by day.
>
> —Rebecca J. Westor

Day 14   Read Hebrews 12:5, 6

Hide and Seek Words ☐

As you read your Bible try to find these hidden words:

"... whom the Lord loveth he chasteneth [trains]"

God Trains You

"What a disobedient sheep! He never would obey my voice. He was always leading the other sheep astray. In love, I broke his leg," the kind shepherd said. "When he is well, he will hear my voice more quickly and follow more closely than any of the other sheep. He has to learn to obey by suffering."

If you disobey God, the Lord Jesus, who is our shepherd, may have to train you through suffering. How much better to obey His voice at once.

The word "chastening" means "child training." Our Father God trains all of His children. He trains us because He loves us. Even when we are walking close to our shepherd, He keeps training us. He wants us to be more useful. If you are having a hard time, it does not always mean that you have been disobedient. But it does mean God loves you!

Day 15   Read Galatians 5:22, 23

Hide and Seek Words ☐

As you read your Bible try to find these hidden words:

"... the fruit of the Spirit is love"

God's Love in Us

When you receive the Lord Jesus as your Savior, God the Holy Spirit comes to live in your heart. As you obey Him others will see that the Holy Spirit is living in you. The things that they see are called the *fruit* of *the Spirit*. Just as the apples on a tree are proof that it is an apple tree, the fruit of the Spirit is proof to others that you belong to God.

The first and most important fruit that others should see in your life is L __ __ __ .

Day 16   Read Psalm 50:10-12

Hide and Seek Words ☐

As you read your Bible try to find these hidden words:

". . . the world is mine"

God Owns It All!

How would you like to have a multi-millionaire for a father? EVERYTHING in Heaven and earth—in the whole universe—is God's. He wants to be your Heavenly Father. What is the only way you can become a child in God's family? (Read John 1:12 if you are not sure.)

What a wonderful Heavenly Father God is! He is able to help you when you ask Him! No matter how many others He must take care of, He will not forget you.

> My Father is rich in houses and lands,
> He holdeth the wealth of the world in His hands!
> Of rubies and diamonds, of silver and gold,
> His coffers are full—He has riches untold.
> I'm a child of the King, a child of the King!
> With Jesus, my Savior, I'm a child of the King.
> —Hattie E. Buell

Day 17   Read Hebrews 1:1, 2

Hide and Seek Words ☐

As you read your Bible try to find these hidden words:

"God ... hath ... spoken ... by his Son"

God Speaks Today

Dan Crawford was a missionary to Africa. One day when he was talking to an African, the man said to him, "We know that God is angry with us because He is silent."

"You think God is silent? Listen," said Mr. Crawford, opening his Bible to the book of Hebrews: " 'God, who ... spoke in time past ... by the prophets, has in these last days spoken unto us by his Son.' "

God has spoken to us through the precious Lord Jesus. Through His Son, God is saying, "I love you so much that I sent My Son to die in your place. Receive Him as your Savior and you will have a home in Heaven with Me." Although it is almost two thousands years ago that God spoke to us by sending His Son, many boys and girls—as well as grown-ups—do not know it even yet. Will you tell someone today?

Day 18   Read Psalm 115:1-3

Hide and Seek Words ☐
As you read your Bible try to find these hidden words:

"... our God is in the heavens"

God Calls

Dear Father, there's the other boy tonight
Who's praying to a god that's made of wood.
He asks it to take care of him till light;
And loves it—but it won't do any good!

What can you do to help the millions of children who worship idols? You can pray for them. You can give to help send missionaries. When you grow up the Lord may give you the great joy of going to them with the good news of the true and living God. Many of the greatest missionaries the world has ever known were called by God when they were boys and girls. If He calls you, answer "Yes." It is a greater work to be a missionary than to be a king!

Day 19 — Read 2 Corinthians 9:7

Hide and Seek Words

As you read your Bible try to find these hidden words:

"God loveth a cheerful giver"

God Gives

Two days ago I picked all the pansy blossoms from my flower bed. Today when I went out to give the plants some water, I found them all covered again with smiling pansies!

"Please pick my flowers," the pansy said,
"Or else I cannot grow;
The more I give, the more I live,
The Father made me so."

So it is with us. God wants us to give ourselves, our time and our money to tell others of the Lord Jesus and to help those in need. If we give to others, He keeps giving us more to give.

Day 20   Read Exodus 20:1, 3

Hide and Seek Words □
As you read your Bible try to find these hidden words:
"...no other gods before me"

One God!

We have been speaking of people who pray to gods made of wood and stone. You know that an idol can't do anything, so you wouldn't be so foolish as to worship it. But there are many other kinds of idols which people worship that are just as sinful as worshiping one made of wood.

An idol is anything that comes between you and God. It is anything you would not be willing to give up for His sake. It may be a person or a thing you love very much, or something that you really want. The Lord Jesus said, "Thou shalt love the Lord thy God with all thy heart, and with all thy soul, and with all thy mind, and with all thy strength." Do you have an idol in your heart?

The dearest idol I have known,
Whatever that idol be;
Help me to cast it from my heart,
And worship only Thee.

Day 21   Read Matthew 6:31-33

Hide and Seek Words ☐

As you read your Bible try to find these hidden words:

"Seek ye first the kingdom of God"

God First!

One time a young fellow left his home to go to the city, where he wanted to become rich. His father told him to SEEK GOD FIRST, but he said, "I will wait until I become rich." In the years when he was making money, he often thought of the verse his father had given him, but he always said to himself, "I will wait until I become wealthy, then I will seek God." Finally, he became an old, white-haired man and had little time left to live. Although he had become rich, he was very unhappy and lonely, for he had not put God first in his life.

If you put God first, He will give you everything else you need. If He wants you to make a lot of money, you will find great joy in using it for His work.

Day 22   Read Philippians 4:6, 7

Hide and Seek Words □

As you read your Bible try to find these hidden words:

"... let your requests be made known"

God Answers

One time an important man called all his workers together for a meeting. He left orders with the man at the door that he was not to be disturbed by anyone. But soon the door opened quietly and a boy went straight to the important man. He said, "Dad, I need some money for lunch, please." While everyone in the meeting waited, the father hunted in his pockets, found some money, and gave it to his son.

God is the Father of all boys and girls who have received His Son Jesus Christ as their Savior. God is never too busy to hear you when you tell Him about the things you need. Isn't that wonderful?

Yesterday He helped me,
Today I have Him near;
Tomorrow is in His own hands—
What cause have I to fear?

Day 23   Read Hebrews 13:5, 6

Hide and Seek Words ☐

As you read your Bible try to find these hidden words:

"I will never leave thee"

God Is Here

Way down deep within their hearts
Everybody's lonesome;
Makes no difference how they smile,
How they live or what their style;
Once in every little while
Everybody's lonesome.

It is a lovely thing to have good friends. The Bible tells us that a friend "loveth at all times." Is that the kind of friend you are to others? God also says, "there is a friend that sticketh closer than a brother." Who is He speaking of? Yes, that friend is the Lord Jesus.

Another way of saying our Hide and Seek Words is, "I will never, never let go of your hand." All through the day and night, the Lord is with you! Aren't you glad for that?

Day 24   Read Job 42:1, 2

Hide and Seek Words ☐
As you read your Bible try to find these hidden words:
"I know that thou canst do every thing"

God Can Do Everything

God has *all* power. *Nothing* is too hard for Him. He is King of kings and Lord of lords. He has all power over *angels*. They do as He tells them. He has all power over *Satan*. Satan can do nothing but what God lets him do. God has all power over *nature*. Even the winds and the waves obey Him. God has all power over *people*. We get our very breath from Him. Isn't it foolish of us to ever want our own way instead of God's way?

It's My delight to answer
    prayer;
Give now to Me your
    every care;
Again, My child, I challenge
    you,
Is anything too hard for ME
    to do?

Day 25   Read 1 Peter 5:6, 7

Hide and Seek Words

As you read your Bible try to find these hidden words:

"... he careth for you"

God Protects

A policeman signaled with his white-gloved hands for the traffic to stop. The vans and taxis all stood still. The boys on bicycles put one foot to the ground. All the work of that busy street was stopped. The people wondered who was coming, and many stretched their necks to see if the king was about to drive through the palace gates.

Then came a surprise! On the empty street so carefully guarded and protected, there walked a mother duck with her little ducklings in single file behind her! There they waddled—all the beaks atwitter and eyes wide open. When they got safely across, the big policeman lowered his arm and traffic moved on once more.

We have an all-powerful protector to take care of us. He is God, our Father. Will you trust Him every day to care for you?

Day 26   Read 1 Peter 1:15, 16

Hide and Seek Words

As you read your Bible try to find these hidden words

"... be ye holy"

Be Like God

"It's a good day to play with our hoops," said Julie to her cousin, Mary. "Look out!" cried Julie. Mary's hoop had run right into a flower bed, crushing several plants. "Oh, dear! They belong to that cross lady," cried Mary.

Just then a big dog bounded across the lawn. The lady appeared at the door, looking very cross. "Say the dog trampled the flowers," whispered Julie.

Mary hesitated, then said: "I'm awful sorry. I didn't mean to. My hoop rolled in." The lady nodded, "Yes, I saw it from the window; I'm glad you were honest."

After that the lady watched for Mary as she came home from school. Sometimes she had flowers for Mary; other times a cookie or an apple. She was soon called "Mary's friend" by the children instead of "the cross old lady!"

Day 27   Read Psalm 141:3, 4

Hide and Seek Words ☐
As you read your Bible try to find these hidden words:
"O Lord... keep the door of my lips"

God Will Help

Keep a watch on your words, my child
For words are wonderful things;
They are sweet like the bee's fresh honey,
Like the bee they have terrible stings!

"I'm mad at Becky; let's not play with her anymore," Kim said to one of her friends. "I hate her, too," the friend replied. "I'm going to pay her back for being mean."

Oh, what tongues we have! God tells us that "the tongue can no man tame; it is an unruly evil, full of deadly poison" (James 3:8). There is only one way to make your tongue speak sweet words. Ask God to guard the "door" of your lips. He will if you give Him not only your tongue but your whole self. As you grow in God's family and trust Him, your words will be more like the bee's honey than like its sting!

Day 28   Read Romans 12:1

Hide and Seek Words ☐
As you read your Bible try to find these hidden words:

"**... present ... a living sacrifice [offering] ... unto God**"

A Gift for God

Why do you enjoy giving gifts to Mother? Isn't it because you love her? There is a gift you can give to God because you love Him. You do not need money or things for this gift. Have you guessed what it is? It is your whole self! God would rather have you than anything else.

Take a piece of wrapping paper. Cut a big circle from it. Then stand on the circle and say, "All that is on this paper, I give to God." Now, what have you given Him? Your feet, your hands, your eyes, ears, tongue, and every other part of yourself, to be His always.

All for Jesus, all for Jesus,
True and faithful may I be;
All for Jesus, all for Jesus,
All for Him who died for me.
                              —E. E. Hewitt

Day 29   Read Proverbs 3:5, 6

Hide and Seek Words ☐

As you read your Bible try to find these hidden words:

"Trust in the Lord with all thine heart"

God Can be Trusted

If you trust and obey your Lord, you can always be sure everything will turn out right, no matter what problems may come.

We have been learning in this booklet how very wonderful our God is; how powerful, how rich, how holy, how awesome, how loving! He is all that we need. He is *the God who is enough.*

Many times you may not understand why something happens but keep on obeying and trusting Him. He has *promised* to guide your life. *He will do it!*

Day 30 — Read John 14:2, 3

Hide and Seek Words □
As you read your Bible try to find these hidden words:

"...a place for you"

God's Home

One of the most precious ways in which God shows His great love for us is by the everlasting HOME He has for us in Heaven. On earth we have wars, sorrows, tears, and all kinds of trouble. But Heaven is our Heavenly Father's house. There we will have joy and happiness forevermore. There will be no more trouble of any kind.

Do you get to Heaven by trying to be good? By praying? By going to church? No! God wants us to do all these things, but there is only one way to Heaven. God's way is to receive the Lord Jesus Christ into your heart as your Savior. If you have done this, then you can be sure you will be in Heaven someday.

God is enough for your life here on earth and for your life in Heaven, too!

Did You Know Jesus Is Called the Lovely One?

Day 1   Read 1 Peter 2:5, 7

Hide and Seek Words ☐

As you read your Bible try to find these hidden words:

"Unto you ... which believe he is precious"

The Lovely One

"What are the loveliest things you know, not counting persons?" a man asked some children one day. They wrote their answers down on paper. One girl wrote: an organ playing, red roofs in trees, rain on your cheeks, red velvet. A boy had on his list: looking into deep clear water, the taste of strawberries, a mounted policeman's horse, a bird singing.

If *you* were asked to name the loveliest *person* you know, whom would you say? Could you say from your heart, "My Savior, Jesus Christ?" He is called in the Bible:

    The rose of Sharon
    The lily of the valleys
    The chiefest among ten thousand
    The one altogether lovely

Is He the "Lovely One" to you? Everyone who really knows the Lord Jesus discovers that He is more lovely and precious than words can tell!

Day 2   Read John 17:3-6

Hide and Seek Words ☐

As you read your Bible try to find these hidden words:

"... the glory which I had with thee"

Before the World Began

Many boys and girls do not know that the Lord Jesus always lived. He lived in Heaven with God the Father *before* He was born in Bethlehem that first Christmas day. Your Hide and Seek Words tell you that Jesus shared glory or honor with His Father. He shared this honor with God in Heaven "before the world was."

Jesus is God the Son. He helped God the Father make this world, yet He became a baby on earth for our sakes. How loving He was to leave His beautiful home where all was joy and happiness. He came to this world to suffer and die for us!

Day 3   Read Genesis 3:21-24

Hide and Seek Words ☐

As you read your Bible try to find these hidden words:

"... the Lord God sent him forth from the garden"

Something Unlovely!

Once there lived, in a beautiful garden, a man and woman who were oh, so very happy. *(You will find this story in the second and third chapters of the Bible.)* But something happened that ended their great joy. They disobeyed God and sinned against Him. It was then necessary for God to send them out of the garden.

It was because of the sin of this first man and woman and because of our sin that Jesus Christ came to earth. He came to die on a cross to take the punishment for all sin. He alone can take away sin. Have you asked the Lord Jesus to take away your sin? If not, will you ask Him just now? When you have done this, write your name and the date below.

Name _____

Date _____

Day 4   Read Isaiah 9:6, 7

Hide and Seek Words ☐

As you read your Bible try to find these hidden words:

"... his name shall be ... The mighty God"

A Wonderful Baby

To those people who knew God's Word, it was no surprise when the Lord Jesus was born. From the very beginning when the first man and woman sinned, God promised to send a Savior. Over 700 hundred years before Jesus came, the Bible tells of His coming in the book of Isaiah. No one but God could have known what was going to happen so far ahead. He even told Isaiah that this Savior would be God—The mighty God. What are some of the other names given to God's Son in Isaiah 9:6?

There was no other good enough
To pay the price of sin;
He only could unlock the gate
Of Heaven and let us in.
　　　　—Cecil F. Alexander

Day 5 — Read Luke 1:30-33

Hide and Seek Words ☐

As you read your Bible try to find these hidden words:

"Fear not, Mary: for thou hast found favor with God"

No One Like Him!

Among the few people who believed God's Word and were looking for the Savior, was a young woman named Mary. One day an angel came to visit her and announced that God was going to give *her* the great honor of being the mother of His Son! Mary was not perfect. She had sinned as all the rest of us have. But she believed God and His Word. Mary was waiting for God to send the Savior He had promised.

Did you know that the baby Jesus was different from any other baby that was ever born? Jesus had an earthly mother, but He had no earthly father. *God was His Father.* The Lord Jesus is the Son of God. He came from Heaven and was born in a human body. Mary's husband, Joseph, helped her take care of God's Son.

Day 6 　　　　　　　Read Matthew 2:1, 2, 11

Hide and Seek Words □
As you read your Bible try to find these hidden words:

"...they...worshipped him"

They Knew Who He Was

Something beautiful happened when Jesus was a baby which showed that He was God. He received worship from wise men who traveled far to see Him.

What a strange sight it must have been to see those wise men in long, rich, flowing robes, bowing low before the child in worship. When you and I see a baby, we sometimes touch his rosy cheeks or his soft chubby hands. But we do not bow our heads to the floor and worship the baby, do we? That would be very wrong, because worship belongs only to God. When wise men bowed to Jesus, it was as if they said, "We are only men, but You are God and man."

Day 7   Read Luke 2:41-52

Hide and Seek Words ☐
As you read your Bible try to find these hidden words:
"I must be about my Father's business"

Are You Like Jesus?

Three things you can learn from the story of the boy Jesus in your Bible verses today (Did you read the story in Luke?):

1. Jesus put God and His work first in His life.
2. He loved to go to God's house or church. (It was then called the *temple*.)
3. He *obeyed* His parents. (This is what *subject unto them* means.)

I should like to have known the boy Jesus,
And at night when I kneel down to pray,
I pray I may grow to be more like Him,
In all that I do ev'ry day.

Day 8   Read John 11:32-36

Hide and Seek Words ☐

As you read your Bible try to find these hidden words:

"Jesus wept"

Jesus Cried Too!

When the Lord Jesus grew up, He often told the people that He was God. But He showed them that He was really a *man*, too. He ate, He slept, He grew tired, He wept, He died as a man. So many times when He spoke of Himself He used the name, "Son of Man."

Your Hide and Seek Words tell you that Jesus wept when His dear friend Lazarus died. When you are in sorrow or trouble He understands. You can be sure of His help too.

Because Jesus was a child and then a man here on this earth, He knows and *understands* your temptation. He was often tempted to do wrong things, just as you are. But He never did wrong! He was "without sin." He is able to help *you* when you are tempted.

Day 9   Read Hebrews 4:14-16

Hide and Seek Words

As you read your Bible try to find these hidden words:

"...tempted...yet without sin"

He Understands You!

Once there was a boy who had been in an accident and lost his right hand. He felt so badly about it that he did not want to see anyone. One day, his father said, "I am going to bring the minister in to see you." But the boy said, "I do not want to see him."

The father brought the minister in anyway. What do you suppose? When the boy looked up he saw that the minister had no right arm; there was only an empty sleeve! He came over to the boy and said, "I haven't any hand either. I lost mine when I was a boy, and I know how it feels." It wasn't hard for the boy to talk with the minister who knew "how it felt."

Nothing can ever happen to us that the Lord cannot understand. He sympathizes with us and loves us even when we are tempted. When temptations come, quickly ask the Lord Jesus to keep you from sinning. He will!

Day 10   Read Mark 3:13, 14

Hide and Seek Words ☐
As you read your Bible try to find these hidden words:

"... that he might send them forth to preach"

Following the Lovely One

The Lord Jesus chose twelve men to help Him in His great work while He was here on earth.

There were twelve disciples
Jesus called to help Him;
Simon Peter, Andrew, James, his brother John;
Philip, Thomas, Matthew,
James, the son of Alphaeus,
Thaddaeus, Simon, Judas, and Bartholomew.

He has called us too, He has called us too;
We are His disciples, I am one and you.
He has called us too, He has called us too;
We are His disciples, we His work must do.

A disciple of Christ is a "learner" and "follower" of Him. Are you His disciple?

Day 11   Read Acts 10:38-40

Hide and Seek Words ☐

As you read your Bible try to find these hidden words:

"... who went about doing good"

Show Him You Love Him

How did Jesus spend His days when He lived here on earth? He went about doing good. You can show others that you love the Lord Jesus by doing good.

"Jan," the minister asked, "do you know how to get to Heaven?" "Oh yes. By being real good!" "No," he replied kindly. "That is not the way to Heaven. No matter how good you are, you cannot earn your way. You can only go God's way. You must receive His Son, Jesus, as your Savior. BUT after you receive Him, because you love Him for having saved you, you should spend your life like Jesus did—going about doing good."

    I cannot work my soul to save,
    For that my Lord has done;
    But I would work like any slave,
    Because I love God's Son!

Day 12   Read Mark 10:13-16

Hide and Seek Words ☐
As you read your Bible try to find these hidden words:

"He took them up in his arms"

All the Children!

A story is told about an artist who painted a beautiful picture of the Lord Jesus. He painted children gathered around Jesus and some of them were sitting upon His knee. When the artist was done he fell asleep. Suddenly he saw someone taking up his brushes and painting over the picture. As he drew close, he saw that it was Jesus. He had painted the faces of the children different colors! They had all been white before, but now they were yellow, brown, black, and red, as well as white. When the artist awakened from the dream, he could not forget the great lesson he had learned. He painted his picture over to look just as it had in his dream.

We know from God's Word that Jesus truly does love *all* boys and girls.

Day 13   Read Matthew 27:35-37

Hide and Seek Words ☐

As you read your Bible try to find these hidden words:

"... they crucified him"

The Greatest Gift

When it came time for Jesus to die, He *willingly* gave His life. Wicked men could not have arrested our Lord if He had not let them. He could have prayed to His Father and He would have sent thousands of angels to rescue Him (Matthew 26:53). He did not need to stay on the cross and die. But if He had come down you could not have been saved. It was when Jesus was hanging on the cross that He took your sins and was punished in *your* place.

Oh, how much it cost the Son of God to give you *free* salvation!

Day 14   Read John 19:28-30

Hide and Seek Words ☐
As you read your Bible try to find these hidden words:
"It is finished"

Once and for All

Jesus cried, "It is finished," while hanging on the cross. This meant that the way of salvation was finished. Our sins were paid for! Oh, how terrible that our sins caused the death of the perfect Son of God! This ought to make us hate sin and run from it!

It pleases God to have you *believe* on His Son and receive Him as your Savior. Then you are saved from sin and have everlasting life. "He that has the Son has life" (1 John 5:12). It is the kind of life which will last forever.

Day 15   Read Matthew 28:5-7

Hide and Seek Words ☐
As you read your Bible try to find these hidden words:
". . . go quickly . . . tell . . . he is risen"

Good News!

Did you ever think of how terrible it would have been if Jesus had stayed dead? Then He could not give you everlasting life! Nothing but a mighty miracle could bring Him back to life. But God worked that mighty miracle. He showed us that He was well pleased with what His Son had done, by raising Him from the dead.

When some women who loved Jesus came to His grave, they found it empty! The angel invited them to look at the place where He had lain and then said, "Go tell." Oh, what wonderful news to tell! Who will *you* tell today?

Go tell He is risen,
Go tell He can save;
Go tell He can meet every need,
Go tell He arose from the grave!

Day 16   Read Luke 24:51-53

Hide and Seek Words ☐

As you read your Bible try to find these hidden words:

"He was... carried up into heaven"

A Real Friend

After the Lord Jesus had risen from the dead He stayed on this earth for forty days. He was seen by His disciples and many others. At one time He was seen by more than 500 people at the same time! We *know* that He is alive.

One day when the Lord Jesus lifted His hands to bless His disciples He went right up to Heaven. He is there today at the right hand of God. What is He doing now? He is praying for you! (Hebrews 7:25)

Jesus is the friend who died for you and who lives to pray for you. You can trust Him to give you everything you need.

Day 17   Read John 14:18-20

Hide and Seek Words ☐

As you read your Bible try to find these hidden words:

"**...because I live, ye shall live also**"

The Caterpillar and You!

A little brown caterpillar felt very sleepy. He began to build a house out of silken threads. Then he lay down cozily and slept and slept. One day he heard the voice of the Heavenly Father saying, "wake up, little butterfly!" His name had been changed. He was no longer a creeping worm but a beautiful butterfly with painted wings.

When you die, the real you (which lives in your body) goes to be with God in Heaven. But your body is put in a grave. When the Lord Jesus comes back He is going to raise your body from the grave. It will be changed to a body like Jesus has. It will again be with the real you. Your body will be perfect. You will not be sick and you will never sin again.

Because Jesus rose from the dead, you will rise too!

Day 18   Read John 14:1-3

Hide and Seek Words □

As you read your Bible try to find these hidden words:

"I will come again"

We Will See Him!

Did you know that Jesus Christ is coming to this earth again some day? That is exactly what He promised when He went back to Heaven. When He does come, the bodies of all the saved people who have died shall come out of the graves. All of God's children will go up to be with the Lord in His Heavenly Home forever. How wonderful that we shall see Him!

Do you know the song, "Jesus Loves Me"? Sing the words below to the same tune.

Christ is coming, this I know,
He, Himself has told me so;
John fourteen, and one, two, three,
Read yourself, and there you'll see.

Yes, He is coming, Yes, He is coming.
Yes, He is coming, the Bible tells me so.

Day 19   Read John 6:35-37

Hide and Seek Words ☐

As you read your Bible try to find these hidden words:

"...he that cometh to me"

He Will Hear You

Two girls arrived home from Sunday school. "Mother," one said, "our teacher told us that we must come to Jesus if we want to be saved from our sins. But how can we come to Him when we cannot see Him?"

"Did you call and ask me to get you a drink of water last night?" replied Mother.

"Yes, Mother."

"Did you see me when you asked me?"

"No, but I knew that you would hear me, and get it for me."

"Well, that is just the way to come to Jesus. You cannot see Him, but He is near and hears every word you say."

The Lord Jesus can hear YOU. You can come to Him and ask Him to save you from YOUR sins. Then you can talk to Him anytime about anything!

Day 20   Read Matthew 16:13-16

Hide and Seek Words ☐
As you read your Bible try to find these hidden words:
"Thou art . . . the Son of the living God"

Who Is He?

Listen to what these people thought of the Savior, Jesus Christ:

Pilate: "I find in him no fault at all" (John 18:38).

Centurion: (a soldier): "Truly this was the Son of God" (Matthew 27:54).

John the Baptist: "Behold the Lamb of God which taketh away the sin of the world" (John 1:29).

Thomas: "My Lord and my God" (John 20:28).

Peter: "Thou art the Christ, the Son of the living God" (Matthew 16:16).

Angel in Heaven: "Unto you is born . . . a Savior, which is Christ the Lord" (Luke 2:11).

Our Heavenly Father: "This is my beloved Son, in whom I am well pleased" (Matthew 17:5).

WHAT DO *YOU* THINK OF THE LORD JESUS? Have you received Him as your Savior? If you never have, do it now and He will come into your heart to stay. Then you can say as Thomas did, "MY Lord and MY God."

Day 21   Read Galatians 2:20

Hide and Seek Words ☐
As you read your Bible try to find these hidden words:
"Christ liveth in me"

He Will Do It!

Here is a very wonderful thing. Christ not only died and rose again, but He now lives *in* me. He lives in YOU if you have received Him as your Savior! The Lord Jesus does not live in those who have not come to Him.

Jesus does not want only a corner of your life. He wants to have *full charge*. If you let Him take charge of your whole life others will know that Jesus is living in you. The things you do will be what He would do. Your thoughts will be pleasing to Him. The words you speak will be kind and loving as His words.

BECAUSE CHRIST LIVES IN YOU, YOU CAN PLEASE GOD.

Day 22   Read Proverbs 23:26

Hide and Seek Words ☐

As you read your Bible try to find these hidden words:

"...give me thine heart"

What Will You Give?

Peter lent a boat
To save Christ from the press.
Martha lent her home
With busy kindliness.

One man lent a colt,
Another lent a room;
Some threw down their clothes,
And Joseph lent a tomb.

What do you have that you can give the Lord Jesus which is greater than any and all of these things? Think as you read the next verse.

Nothing have I to lend—
No boat, no house, no lands;
Lord, here is my life—myself,
I place it in Your hands.

Jesus gave Himself for you; will you now give yourself to Him? That is the thing He wants most of all after you receive Him as your Savior.

Lord Jesus, I do give myself to You for always.

Name_____

Date_____

Day 23   Read John 1:40-42

Hide and Seek Words ☐
As you read your Bible try to find these hidden words:
"... he brought him to Jesus"

The Ant, Andrew, and You!

One time a man put an ant on top of a piece of candy on the table. As soon as the ant had a taste of how good the sugar was, he hurried down the table leg and off to his ant friends. He had his own way of telling them there was something sweet and good on the table. When he turned to go back there was a long trail of ants following him. He led them all to the piece of candy. How they enjoyed the feast!

Andrew had some good news to share too! As soon as he found the Lord Jesus, Andrew hurried to tell his brother, Peter.

Is Jesus your Savior? Then you should be busy telling others about Him. Are there some in your family who do not know Him and love Him? How about the boys and girls you play with at school? Tell someone today so that they too will know that Jesus died for them!

Day 24   Read John 15:12-14

Hide and Seek Words ☐
As you read your Bible try to find these hidden words:

"...if ye do whatsoever I command you"

A Friend of Jesus

It was a very special day at Sunday school. The children sat together on the platform. They were going to stand and say the Bible verses they had learned. Pam felt very proud as she stood and said her verse, "Be not forgetful to entertain strangers." Next to her sat Eric, a new boy. "I wish I didn't have to sit next to him," whispered Pam with a frown. Kristi sat on the other side of Eric. Her verse was, "Be ye kind." When she saw Pam's frown, she thought, *I guess she's forgotten to be kind to strangers. I'll try to be kind to Eric.* Kristi didn't know how to begin, so she just smiled at Eric and he smiled back. His bright eyes watched her closely after that. How glad he was to have a friend!

How did Kristi show she was a true friend of the Lord Jesus? (Read the Hide and Seek Words to see if your answer is correct.)

Day 25   Read 1 John 3:16-18

Hide and Seek Words ☐

As you read your Bible try to find these hidden words:

"... let us ... love ... in deed and in truth"

I Love You, Mother

"I love you, Mother," said little John;
Then forgetting his work, his cap went on.
And he was off to the garden swing,
And she had the wood and water to bring.

"I love you, Mother," said rosy Nell;
"I love you more than tongue can tell."
Then she teased and pouted half the day,
Till her mother was glad when she went to play.

"I love you, Mother," said little Nan;
"Today I'll help you all I can;
My doll and playthings I know will keep!"
Then she rocked the baby fast asleep.

Stepping softly, she brought the broom,
And swept the floor and tidied the room.
Busy and happy all day was she,
Helpful and good as a child could be.

"I love you, Mother," again they said,
Three little children going to bed.
How do you think the mother guessed
Which of them really loved her best?

—Joy Allison

How can you show others you love them? (Read your Hide and Seek Words for the answer.)

Day 26   Read Matthew 25:22, 23

Hide and Seek Words ☐

As you read your Bible try to find these hidden words:

"... thou hast been faithful over a few things"

Little Jobs First!

So often it is in the *little things* that you can show your love and obedience to the Lord Jesus. Do you scrape the dishes cheerfully? When you sweep the floor, do you clean in the corners? Or, do you think, *Oh, no one will notice there, so I'll just skip it*? When Mother is tired there are many little things you can do for her. Do you remember to do them, and do them with a smile? The Lord sees your work. He never gives big jobs to those who do not learn to do the little things first. *But* if you are faithful in a few things, He may some day trust you with many and big things.

> God has no end of people
> Who would be prophets and kings,
> But what He needs is volunteers,
> To do the little things.

What can you do for the Lord Jesus today?

Day 27   Read 1 Thessalonians 5:15-18

Hide and Seek Words ☐
As you read your Bible try to find these hidden words:
"Rejoice [be filled with joy] evermore"

Bubbling Over!

If you have received the Lord Jesus as your Savior from sin, He wants you to be bubbling over with JOY. You have this joy when you obey God, and ask forgiveness when you fail to obey. This joy comes from knowing God is pleased with your life.

How do you spell *joy*? Let the J stand for Jesus; the O stand for Others; and the Y stand for You. Oh, how selfish we often are. Selfish people are always unhappy. If you want to "rejoice evermore" think of:

Jesus
Others
You

Day 28   Read Proverbs 3:5, 6

Hide and Seek Words ☐

As you read your Bible try to find these hidden words:

"... **lean not unto thine own understanding**"

God Will Show You

Mother let Shannon have the fun of picking out a new doll for a birthday present. Shannon *insisted* on buying the first one she saw. After Shannon had her own way she saw some dolls that were much more beautiful. It was a sad little girl who heard Mother say, as she picked up one of those dolls, "This was the kind I *wanted* to get you."

We often want our own way instead of God's. But His way is always so much better. God tells us that we do not know how to choose the right things. Ask God and He will show you what to do.

Day 29 Read 2 Corinthians 3:17, 18

Hide and Seek Words □

As you read your Bible try to find these hidden words:

"We all . . . are changed"

What Do You Look Like?

Do you enjoy having your picture taken? When the Lord Jesus lived, there were no photographers. So we do not have any true picture of Him. The pictures we have of Jesus show the way the artists *thought* He looked. We know that His face must have been very loving, for what is in a person's heart shows on his face.

> We have no picture of the Christ
> To show His gentle face;
> But you and I can wear a smile,
> And brighten every place!
> The world needs not to see His face,
> For it has you and me;
> If we but do His holy will,
> In us the Christ they'll see.

Do others see the Lord Jesus in *your* face? Keep following Him and they will!

Day 30 Read 1 Peter 1:8, 9

Hide and Seek Words

As you read your Bible try to find these hidden words:

"Whom having not seen, ye love"

Love Him!

You may like to collect pictures of people you love. One time a little girl was killed in an accident. The policeman found a locket around her neck. In it was written, "Whom having not seen, I love." These words were about the Lord Jesus. He was the one she loved but had never seen. She did not guess when she put this verse in her locket that she would see Jesus so soon and be with Him forever! How happy she must have been when she looked into His face.

Just fall in love with Jesus,
He'll take you as you are,
He's altogether lovely,
The Bright and Morning Star.
He never will forsake you,
He'll save you from your sin,
And take you home to Heaven,
Just fall in love with Him!

Have you "fallen in love" with the Lord Jesus, the lovely one?

Lord Jesus, Teach Us How to Pray

Day 1   Read Luke 11:1-4

Hide and Seek Words ☐

As you read your Bible try to find these hidden words:

"Lord, teach us to pray"

God Answers!

Mrs. Taylor was writing a book.

"I'm writing a book, too, Mrs. Taylor," Sherri said. "It's about my answers to prayer."

"Do you get answers to prayer that you can write in a book?" asked Mrs. Taylor.

"Yes, I do," Sherri said brightly, "lots of them. I began writing them down last summer."

Mrs. Taylor was very interested. "How many answers have you had in those eight months?"

"Well, I didn't get them all written down, but I do have 150 in my book," Sherri answered.

You, too, can have your prayers answered! Learn more about prayer by looking each day for the Hide and Seek Words in your Bible and by reading a page from this book.

Day 2   Read John 1:11-13

Hide and Seek Words ☐

As you read your Bible try to find these hidden words:

"... power to become the sons [children] of God"

Special! For God's Children

This little booklet about prayer is written for you if you are a child of God. Children in God's family can expect to get their prayers answered. Perhaps you are not sure whether you are in God's family or not. You can be sure right now. First, you need to see that *you* have sinned (Romans 3:23). Second, you need to know that the Lord Jesus died on the cross to take away your sin (1 Peter 2:24). Third, you need to receive (or take) Jesus Christ as your very own Savior, as John 1:12 tells you. You can tell the Lord Jesus right now that you receive Him as your Savior. He will hear you. The moment you do this you become part of God's family.

Write your name here if you are a child of God.

_____

Day 3   Read John 14:13-15

Hide and Seek Words ☐

As you read your Bible try to find these hidden words:

". . . ask . . . in my name"

Jesus Made The Way

Have you noticed that at the end of our prayers we say, "for Jesus' sake," or "in Jesus' name"? Why do we do this? It is because we cannot speak to God in any other way except through His Son, the Lord Jesus Christ.

We are sinful. We cannot come to a holy God in our sins and ask Him for favors. But the Lord Jesus is without sin. It is only because He died for our sins that we can come to God. When we come to Him in Jesus' name God delights to hear and answer us. We can be sure that He will forgive our sins because of the Lord Jesus. Don't let it be just "words" when you say, "for Jesus' sake," for just words do not count with God. He looks on the heart to see if you really mean it.

Day 4   Read Matthew 7:7, 8

Hide and Seek Words ☐

As you read your Bible try to find these hidden words:

"Ask, and it shall be given you"

Doesn't God Know?

Through prayer, you ask God for things you need. But why must you do this? He already knows all about you; He knows what you need. So why must you ask Him? One reason is that it would make you very, very selfish if God always gave you good things without your even asking Him or thanking Him. If you need something, don't you think it is only right that you should ask God, since He owns everything? But *most important*, by asking God for what you need you show that you believe His Word and are obeying Him. Believing what God says pleases Him.

Day 5   Read Psalm 66:18-20

Hide and Seek Words ☐
As you read your Bible try to find these hidden words:

"God hath heard . . . my prayer"

Sin Stops God's Answers

Two sisters were praying at night. One jumped into bed at once. The other waited quietly. The first asked, "What are you waiting for, Ruth?" Her sister answered, "Our teacher suggested that after we speak to God we wait for Him to speak to us."

"Did God say anything to you tonight?" her sister asked.

"You know," Ruth replied, "we asked God to bless our friends. God made me think of Sandy and the fuss we had today. While I was waiting, God said, 'Tell her you are sorry.'"

If you are one of God's children, but are doing things you *know* are sinful, you cannot expect the Lord to hear your prayers. But if you ask Him to show you the wrong things in your life, He will. When you make them right as much as you can, you may be sure He will hear and answer you.

Day 6   Read Luke 18:9-14

Hide and Seek Words □

As you read your Bible try to find these hidden words:

"Two men went... to pray"

The Prayer That Pleases God

Many times boys and girls say that they haven't done anything bad, but they tell about a boy at school or a girl who lives next door who does terrible things! They are like the Pharisee—the proud man Jesus told about—in the Bible verses you read today. The Pharisee began his prayer by telling God how good he was and how thankful that he was not like the sinful tax collector who was called a publican. But, it was the publican's prayer that pleased God! The publican admitted he was a sinner. He knew he wasn't good enough to come to God. He went away knowing that his sins were forgiven.

Oh, don't ever make the mistake of thinking you are good enough to come to God as you are. There is no other way but through Christ your Savior.

Day 7 — Read Mark 11:25, 26

Hide and Seek Words

As you read your Bible try to find these hidden words:

"...when ye stand praying, forgive"

If You Forgive

We so often sin against God—all of us. We need His forgiveness. Your Bible verses tell that when you come to God to pray for forgiveness of your sins, you must also forgive anyone who has wronged you. If you keep an ugly feeling in your heart for someone, it takes away that sweet peace that the Holy Spirit put there. The prayer below was written by a girl when she was not much older than you. Will you make it your prayer too?

Let me be forgiving!
If someone is unkind.
Help me with a little song
To put it out of mind.

Let me with a sunny smile
Send it right away.
For angry thoughts can darken
The brightest kind of day.

Day 8   Read Psalm 106:1, 2

Hide and Seek Words ☐
As you read your Bible try to find these hidden words:
"Praise ye the Lord"

Much To Be Happy About!

Before you ask God for anything, thank and praise Him first, for:

Prayer and praises go in pairs,
Those who praise have joyful prayers.

If you have Jesus Christ as your own Savior, you have so much to be happy about. Praise Him that you are saved and your sins forgiven. Praise Him that you are "born again" into God's family and have eternal life. Thank Him that you are on the way to Heaven where you will share in God's great riches and be joyful all the time. Praise God that He is taking care of you right now and giving you the things you need—the precious Bible, parents, friends, home, and church.

Day 9 — Read Philippians 4:6, 7

Hide and Seek Words ☐

As you read your Bible try to find these hidden words:

"...by prayer...with thanksgiving"

Don't Forget!

Do you have any pets? Josh had pet rabbits. One day they got out of their pen. Josh scurried around and caught all of them but one. He felt badly about that one; then he remembered to pray!

Josh knelt by the bushes and asked God to help him. Just as he opened his eyes, what do you suppose he saw? Yes, the rabbit! It was running right toward him. He caught it in his hands and put it back in the pen. He was so happy that he knelt down in the same spot and thanked God!

Are *you* praying to God and getting answers to your prayers? Don't forget to thank Him when the answers come. It is even better to thank Him *before* the answer comes. That shows you really believe God is going to keep His promises.

Day 10   Read Ephesians 6:18-20

Hide and Seek Words ☐

As you read your Bible try to find these hidden words:

"... praying always ... for all saints [children of God]"

What Shall We Ask?

After thanking and praising the Lord in your prayer, what should you ask Him for? For *yourself*, that you may live to please Him since you have become one of His children. For any in your *family* who do not love the Lord Jesus. For *any who are unkind* to you. Pray for the *missionaries*, your *Sunday school*, and *church*. For *those who are in trouble*. Bring all your needs to God in prayer. Talk to Him about everything.

Especially, will you pray for the millions of children who do not know our Savior? Do the boys and girls you play with know Jesus? Bring someone to know the Savior today!

Pray, pray, pray; the Bible says to pray...
That boys and girls who never heard
Be plainly told the blessed Word.
Oh, who will pray? Oh, will YOU pray?

Day 11   Read Psalm 91:14-16

Hide and Seek Words ☐

As you read your Bible try to find these hidden words:

"I will be with him in trouble"

Jesus Makes Things Right

"Lord, please take care of me tonight," Billy prayed, as he said his evening prayers. "I can take care of myself in the daytime." What was wrong with Billy's prayer? Yes, he needed the Lord to take care of him just as much in the daytime as in the night! You need the Lord Jesus to protect and guide and help you each moment of the day and night, too. He wants you to pray to Him always, and especially when you are in trouble. Are you having a hard time with your lessons? Are you in trouble because of wrongdoing? Do your school friends not want to play with you? Talk to the Lord Jesus in prayer about your needs. He knows how to make things right, and He will!

> In trials of every kind, praise God, I always find,
> A little talk with Jesus makes it right, all right.

Day 12   Read Mark 11:22-24

Hide and Seek Words ☐

As you read your Bible try to find these hidden words:

"**. . . when ye pray, believe**"

Only Believe!

When you put your letter in the mailbox did you really *believe* it would go to your friend whose name was written on the envelope? Of course you did! When you got on the bus and paid your fare, did you *believe* the bus would take you where you wanted to go? Of course! Do you *really believe* when you pray to God in Jesus' name that He will answer your prayers? Do you? God is much more able to do what He promises than either the mailman or the bus driver! Sometimes, very foolishly, we do not trust God to do what He says He will. "Without faith it is impossible to please him." Please Him by believing!

Only believe, only believe,
All things are possible, only believe;
Only believe, only believe,
All things are possible, only believe.

—Paul Rader

Day 13   Read 1 Samuel 1:9-11 and 27

Hide and Seek Words ☐

As you read your Bible try to find these hidden words:

"For this child I prayed"

Not Too Hard for God!

In the Bible we learn about a lady by the name of Hannah. She was often sad because she and her husband had no child. One day when she went to the temple, which was their church, she cried and prayed for God to send them a baby boy. Hannah promised that if He would, she would give this child to the Lord.

God, who has all power, sent the baby. Do you suppose it was a girl? Oh no, God sent her just what she had asked for—a boy. Hannah *kept her promise to God* too and gave Samuel (the boy's name) to work for the Lord. Even as a small boy Samuel prayed to God and God talked to him, too! You can read about him in 1 Samuel 3:1-10.

There's nothing too hard for Thee, dear Lord
Nothing too hard for Thee,
Nothing, no nothing;
There's nothing too hard for Thee.

Day 14   Read James 4:1-3

Hide and Seek Words ☐

As you read your Bible try to find these hidden words:

"Ye... receive not, because ye ask amiss"

A Prayer Warning

Two little birds quarreled over a worm,
For neither wished to divide;
While they sputtered and jeered,
That worm disappeared,
Not waiting for them to decide!

It is not only birds that are sometimes selfish. Love of self is one of the greatest sins among boys and girls. Think about what *you* do. Do you always want to be first in a game? Do you want the biggest piece of cake and the best toys to play with, instead of letting others have them? Do you want your own way? Love of yourself will grow and grow unless you let the Lord Jesus rule your life.

Remember, if you pray for things which are only for your selfish self, and not to honor God, you cannot expect Him to answer.

Day 15 — Read Romans 8:26, 27

Hide and Seek Words

As you read your Bible try to find these hidden words:

"We know not what we should pray for"

Your Prayer Helper

Sometimes you do not know what you should pray for; but the Holy Spirit who lives in the hearts of God's children knows. He will pray through you as you trust Him to guide you in your prayers. The Holy Spirit is God, and He knows what is best for you.

When you are ill you are anxious to get well again! But sometimes God has wonderful lessons to teach you when you are sick. It is often then that you get to know and love Him better than ever before. Here is a good prayer to pray when you are sick.

Dear Lord, I am Your little child
And now I'm sick and sad:
If You will only say a word,
Then I'll be well and glad.
But if it should not be Your will,
Just stay real close—
I'll love You still.

Day 16   Read 1 John 5:13-15

Hide and Seek Words ☐

As you read your Bible try to find these hidden words:

"... ask ... according to his will"

A Prayer Promise

In your prayers, if you ask anything which is God's will, you can be sure of receiving the answer. Sometimes you may be puzzled to know whether a thing is God's will or not. How will you find out? First, *by God's promises* in His Word, the Bible. That is one reason why you must read the Bible. Second, you will find God's will *by the Holy Spirit* who lives in the heart of every saved person. Listen for His quiet voice in your heart. He is your guide. When God does not show you His will at once, wait and trust Him. He will show you when He sees best.

> Being in doubt, I say,
> "Lord, make it plain!
> Which is the true way?
> Which would be vain?
> I am not wise to know
> Nor sure of foot to go;
> My blind eyes cannot see
> What is so clear to You,
> Lord, make it clear to me."

Day 17   Read Luke 22:39-43

Hide and Seek Words ☐
As you read your Bible try to find these hidden words:

"...not my will, but thine"

Three Answers

I believe God answers prayer
I am sure God answers prayer
I have proved God answers prayer,
Glory to His name.

Many, many boys and girls are having their prayers answered. Are you, too? God has three ways of answering your prayers.

They are:

1 Yes
2 No
3 Wait

It is wonderful when He answers your prayers soon; but sometimes He sees it is best for you to "wait awhile" before He sends the answer. When He says, "No," that means it is not His will or plan for you. It means also that He has something better than the thing you asked for! You must *want* God's will, whatever it may be, when you pray.

Day 18   Read Colossians 4:1-3

Hide and Seek Words ☐

As you read your Bible try to find these hidden words:

"Continue in prayer"

Too Much Hurry!

Stacy got so tired of waiting for those little chicks to hatch out of the eggs! So she decided to help them out. She opened all the shells. But oh! She soon discovered that the air struck the baby chicks too soon and killed all but one!

Matt was out in Mother's rose garden. When he came in Mother asked what he had been doing. "Oh, I saw a nice rosebud and I blossomed it," he said. Mother went out to look and she found the rose spoiled. If Matt had left it in the sun, it would have blossomed by itself and been so beautiful. He had spoiled it by being in too much of a hurry!

God does not always answer our prayers right away. He wants to teach us patience and trust. We can be sure He *will* answer, when it is His own best time. Let's not spoil the answer by being in a hurry!

Day 19   Read 1 Thessalonians 5:17, 18

Hide and Seek Words ☐

As you read your Bible try to find these hidden words:

"Pray without ceasing"

Doing Your Part

Two girls were on their way to school one day. They had not started as early as usual, and were afraid they would be late. They were Christians, so one said, "Let's stop here and ask God not to let us be late." But the other girl said, "No, I'll run as fast as I can. And *while I'm running* I'll ask God to help me get there in time." Which girl do you think was right?

Sometimes the Lord uses you to answer your own prayers. When you pray, if there is something you can do about it, you should do it! God will not do for you what you can do for yourself.

Are you learning to pray about everything? That is the happiest way to live!

Day 20   Read James 5:16-18

Hide and Seek Words ☐

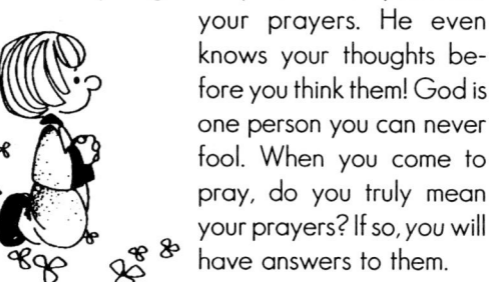

As you read your Bible try to find these hidden words:

**"He prayed earnestly...
he prayed again"**

Pray With All Your Heart!

To say our prayers is not to pray
Unless we mean the words we say,
Unless we think to whom we speak
And with our hearts His blessing seek.

Then let us, when we come to pray,
Not only heed the words we say,
But let us seek with earnest care
To truly think and mean our prayer.

God, who sees you through and through and knows everything about you, knows if you mean your prayers. He even knows your thoughts before you think them! God is one person you can never fool. When you come to pray, do you truly mean your prayers? If so, you will have answers to them.

Day 21   Read Matthew 18:19, 20

Hide and Seek Words ☐

As you read your Bible try to find these hidden words:

"...gathered together in my name"

A Family That Prayed

Jackie and Gladys Williams lived in a home where their mother and father prayed and read the Bible with them. They had a dog named Spot. During their prayer time, morning and evening, they taught Spot to put his two front paws on a chair as though he were praying too! When the family had to move, they gave their dog to Mrs. Roberts.

Mrs. Roberts could not imagine what Spot was up to, when each morning he put his two front paws on a chair and made a strange noise. When she met Mrs. Williams she asked her. With a surprised look, Jackie and Gladys' mother explained, "It is Spot's way of 'praying'." Mrs. Roberts began to think that it would be a good thing for their family to pray too. So they started family prayers—all because of Spot!*

*Adapted from "Happy Hours with Little Folks"

Day 22   Read Hebrews 13:5, 6

Hide and Seek Words ☐
As you read your Bible try to find these hidden words:
"The Lord is my helper"

Make It Right!

One time Michael broke a neighbor's window. He ran to his father, crying, "What shall I do?" "Do?" said his father. "Tell Mr. Morgan about it. Ask him what you must pay; then pay it like a man." "I-I thought that all I had to do was to ask God to forgive me," Michael said.

Your loving Father, God, is always ready to forgive your wrongs when you confess them to Him (1 John 1:9). But whenever there is something you can do to right a wrong you have done, He expects you to do it! If you have taken something which did not belong to you, return it or pay for it. If you hurt someone, tell him you are sorry. This will not be easy. But the Lord will be with you and help you say, "I'm sorry. I will do whatever I can to make it right."

Day 23 Read John 6:9-14

Hide and Seek Words ☐

As you read your Bible try to find these hidden words:

"Jesus . . . when he had given thanks"

Thank You, Lord!

How would you like to have been the boy with the lunch? In Jesus' hands his bread and fish were changed into enough food to feed more than 5,000 people! There were even 12 baskets full of "left-overs"! "I'm sure glad I gave my lunch," I can hear him say. "Just look what I would have missed if I hadn't let Jesus have it."

What did Jesus do first? He "gave thanks." It is His wish too, that you thank Him for your food and the other good things He gives you. Ask if you can say this prayer before your meals.

> Dear Lord, we thank You for this food,
> We pray You'll bless it to our good;
> And help us live Your name to praise,
> In all we do, through all our days. Amen.

Day 24   Read Psalm 34:1-4

Hide and Seek Words ☐
As you read your Bible try to find these hidden words:
"... he delivered me from all my fears"

Safe with God

"Let us travel with the Christians. If we are with them we shall be safe, because they *pray* and their God *protects* them." These were Chinese soldiers speaking. In the next room three women missionaries were preparing for a long, long trip across the desert. The women were in danger of robbers, lack of food and water, sickness and many others things. *But* they trusted in God. They prayed to Him about everything and He kept them from fear. God sends His angels to protect all who trust and love Him (Psalm 34:7). With angels around us and the Lord always ready to hear our prayers, we are well cared for, don't you think?

Day 25　　　　　　　　　　Read Mark 10:13, 14

Hide and Seek Words

As you read your Bible try to find these hidden words:

"Suffer [let] the little children...come"

Everybody Ought to Know!

There was a little Hindu girl,
She was about so tall;
Each morning she had rice to eat,
But did not eat it all.

Oh, no! She took a little out,
About so much, I think,
And gave it to a wooden god
That could not eat nor drink.

She laid it down before his face,
And said a little prayer;
The idol could not see nor hear,
For her he did not care.

She did the very best she knew,
'Twas what her mother taught her;
She thought the idol, old and grim,
Could help her little daughter.

I want that little Hindu girl
To love our Lord in glory,
And I'll do all I can to help
Send her "the old, old story."

You can help by *praying* for children of other lands who do not know Jesus.

Day 26   Read John 3:1-3

Hide and Seek Words ☐
As you read your Bible try to find these hidden words:

"Except a man be born again"

A Man Who Prayed

When George Mueller was young, he was not a good boy. He was not truthful. He took money which did not belong to him and was once put in jail. George tried to live better but failed. He needed to be "born again."

It was a happy day for George Mueller when he went to a Bible class one evening with a friend. There he heard how to be saved from his sins. Gladly he received Christ as his Savior and was "born again" into God's family. After that day, George Mueller received many, many answers to prayer.

Whether you have sinned little or much, you need Christ's own life in you to make you good. That is the only real way to be good. You receive Christ's own life when you trust Jesus as your Savior. This new life begins to grow and you become more and more like Christ.

Day 27   Read John 15:7, 8

Hide and Seek Words ☐

As you read your Bible try to find these hidden words:

"If ye abide . . . it shall be done"

He Prayed for Others!

After Mr. Mueller was saved, the Lord Jesus was very real to him. He wanted people to know that God would answer *their* prayers. The Lord led him to start an orphanage for boys and girls in England. Mr. Mueller didn't have a penny to do this with, but he knew God was rich. So he decided not to ask anyone for money, but just pray to God for it.

The orphanage opened with only one child there, but more boys and girls came until there were over two thousand! Mr. Mueller had to rent more houses; then build bigger ones to take care of so many children. Sometimes gifts of just pennies were sent or given to him by people who loved the Lord. Other times gifts of thousands of dollars came. During his lifetime he received over seven million dollars in answer to prayer for the children!

Day 28   Read 1 John 3:22-23

Hide and Seek Words ☐
As you read your Bible try to find these hidden words:
"... we receive of him"

On Time!

What would you do if you had to feed over 2,000 boys and girls and didn't have any money or food? One time there was no food at all in the house for breakfast and Mr. Mueller had no money to buy any. He had the children all come in and sit down at the tables. Then he thanked God for their food, as he always did. But there was no food—the tables were empty!

Suddenly—someone was at the door! There stood the baker. "I couldn't sleep last night," he said. "The Lord asked me to get up and bake you some bread for the orphans." There before their eyes, was enough hot bread for all. The bell rang again! Who do you think it was this time? The milkman! "My milk-cart has broken down right in front of your orphanage. I would like to give you my cans of milk," he said. Oh, what joy! God heard their prayers and had sent their breakfast!

Day 29   Read Psalm 37:3-5

Hide and Seek Words ☐

As you read your Bible try to find these hidden words:

"... he shall give thee"

God Loves to Give

"I wish God would answer my prayers like He does yours, George Mueller," said three-year-old Abbie. Taking her on his lap, Mr. Mueller repeated to her God's promise, "What things soever ye desire, when ye pray *believe* that ye receive them, and ye shall have them."

"Now, Abbie, what is it you want to ask God for?" She answered, "Some wool." So together they prayed for some wool for Abbie. Then she went about her play.

The next day Abbie was filled with joy and delight to receive a package by mail addressed to her. Guess what was in it! Many, many little balls of yarn! While away on a visit her teacher had found the wool. She thought Abbie might like it and sent the box to her. Though Abbie lived to be 80 years old, she never forgot this first answer to prayer.

Day 30 — Read Mark 6:45, 46

Hide and Seek Words

As you read your Bible try to find these hidden words:

"He departed . . . to pray"

Jesus Prays

When the Lord Jesus was here on this earth, He had no home of His own. He had no room where He could be alone to pray. But this did not keep Him from praying. He loved to talk to His Father, and sometimes went into the mountains to pray. One time He spent all night in prayer. He prayed when He was baptized (Luke 3:21) and before they took Him to nail Him to the cross (Mark 14:32). He prayed for His disciples and for all of us who would believe on Him (John 17:9, 20).

There is something still more wonderful. *The Lord Jesus is praying for you now. He ever lives to pray for us* (Hebrews 7:25). The long word "intercession" means *praying for us.* Oh, that we might love such a wonderful Savior more and more!

I Think the Holy Spirit Must Be Like a Dove

Day 1 — Read John 14:16-18

Hide and Seek Words ☐

As you read your Bible try to find these hidden words:

"I will come to you"

My Closest Friend

Chad had the measles. He was lonely having to stay in bed all day while the other boys played. But one day a dove flew onto the sill of his open window. The dove never left as long as Chad was ill. "He makes me think of our nearest friend, the Holy Spirit," said Chad's mother. "You know before the Lord Jesus went back to Heaven He promised to send us another Comforter, His other self, the Holy Spirit. He is our *Stay-Within Friend*. He lives in the heart of everyone who has received the Lord Jesus as Savior."

"I'm ashamed that I have been lonely," decided Chad. "I have my very closest friend living right in my heart!"

Day 2

Read John 16:13, 14

Hide and Seek Words ☐

As you read your Bible try to find these hidden words:

"He, the Spirit of truth, is come"

Very Real!

When the Lord Jesus was on earth the Holy Spirit came to Him. He appeared like a dove so that others could see Him coming from Heaven (John 1:32). But the Holy Spirit is really a *person*. He is God!

> O God the Father, O God the Son,
> O God the Spirit, Three in One;
> We worship You now,
> We bring You our love,
> Join in the praises of hosts above.

Kenny wondered, *If the Holy Spirit is a person, why can't I see Him?* Then he remembered—he could not see the wind that made his boat go skimming over the water. Yet the wind was real. He could not see the pain when he skinned his knee, but it was real just the same. Kenny decided, *A lot of what I cannot see must be more real than what I can see!* He was beginning to understand about the Holy Spirit.

Day 3   Read 1 Corinthians 6:19, 20

Hide and Seek Words

As you read your Bible try to find these hidden words:

"... the Holy Ghost [Holy Spirit] which is in you"

My Heart House

"I'm glad I know the Holy Spirit is a person and that He is God." Carol spoke half aloud. "But I think the most wonderful thing is what our teacher told us today. I heard it very clearly. She said, *'The Holy Spirit lives in the heart of every boy and girl who has truly received Christ as his Savior.'* "

Yes, Carol was right! God's Word says so! He is our *Stay-Within* Friend!

I am a house in which God lives,
A house to which He came
When I believed that Christ forgave
My sins in His dear Name
I am a house in which He stays,
My best and truest Friend;
He'll never leave me all my days,
And keep me to the end.

Day 4   Read Romans 14:17

Hide and Seek Words ☐

As you read your Bible try to find these hidden words:

"...joy in the Holy Ghost [Holy Spirit]"

A Smile on the Inside

Tony always made others laugh! His class at school was just not the same when Tony was absent.

One day Andrew asked a very strange question. "Are you smiling on the inside, too, Tony?"

"What do you mean?"

"Well, are you really happy in your heart?"

Tony's eyes became even brighter. "Sure am, Andrew. You know, I told you before that I asked the Lord Jesus to forgive my sins. Well, when He forgave me, His Holy Spirit came to live in my heart. He is the one who makes me happy inside."

"Tony," Andrew said, "you've got to help me receive Jesus, too. The bad things I've done are making me *miserable!*"

Day 5   Read 2 Peter 1:20, 21

Hide and Seek Words ☐

As you read your Bible try to find these hidden words:

"... moved by the Holy Ghost [Holy Spirit]"

A Miracle Book

The Holy Ghost (another name for God the Holy Spirit) has written a book. It is the world's treasure book, the Bible. He had many secretaries. He told them what to write. The things they wrote are *the very words of God*.

The Holy Spirit used many different persons to write down God's message: a tent-maker, a tax collector, a shepherd who became a king, a farmer, a fisherman and many others. The Bible belongs to all people in all times and in all nations. Boys and girls in the farthermost corner of the earth have just as much right to it as you!

The Bible is a miracle book. It is from God to you. It is your guidebook to Heaven.

>Its pages, through ages,
>Have brought salvation free;
>Receive it, believe it, the B-I-B-L-E.

Day 6 — Read John 14:23-27

Hide and Seek Words ☐

As you read your Bible try to find these hidden words:

"The Holy Ghost... shall teach you all things"

The Key to God's Word

"If the Bible is my guidebook, I don't see why it's so hard to understand," complained David. "I'd rather play!"

"That's because you need the key to open it," answered Dad.

"A key? What kind of key would open the Bible?"

"The key to the Bible is the one who wrote it—the Holy Spirit. God has locked all the goodness inside, but He has given you the key. You can never understand the Bible unless the Holy Spirit teaches you. He is a great teacher. Ask *Him* to give you understanding as you read and study God's Word."

Day 7   Read John 3:5-8

Hide and Seek Words ☐

As you read your Bible try to find these hidden words:

"Ye must be born again"

A New Life for You

Sam put up a scarecrow to scare away the birds from his garden! But he didn't fool the birds even one little bit! They perched all over the scarecrow and even built a nest in his hat! It almost seemed they knew the scarecrow didn't have any life in him. He was just a stuffed dummy!

You were born with life inside of you but it is not the right kind of life for Heaven. The Holy Spirit shows you that you are a sinner. You need to have your sins washed away by the blood of Christ. You need a new life within. Have *you* been born again? The *Holy Spirit* causes you to be born again when you receive Christ. The *Holy Spirit lives in your heart* after you have been born again. You may look the same on the outside, but inside you have the Holy Spirit and a new life.

Day 8 — Read Revelation 22:16, 17

Hide and Seek Words ☐

As you read your Bible try to find these hidden words:

"...the Spirit and the bride say, Come"

The Queen Prayed

"Are you a Christian, my dear," asked Queen Victoria.

"Oh yes, your Majesty," answered the girl.

"How do you know you are?" asked the Queen.

"Oh, because I've been baptized and joined the church."

The Queen made no answer to this, but prayed:

"Lord, show this dear young girl that without a change inside of her she can never become a true Christian. Show her that no work she can do will save her soul. This I ask in the name of the Lord Jesus Christ."

While the Queen prayed, the Holy Spirit showed the girl that she needed to be born again into God's family. That is one of the works of the Holy Spirit—to show us we need to be saved from our sin. The great Queen Victoria was very happy when her young friend received Christ as her Savior.

Day 9   Read John 3:35, 36

Hide and Seek Words ☐

As you read your Bible try to find these hidden words:

". . . hath everlasting life"

It's in the Book!

Irish Patrick asked, "And how is it, Mother, that you're looking all sad this morning? Just last night it was happy you were because you took Jesus as your Savior."

"Oh, Son, Son, I lost all the good feelin'. I thought last night as to how it's everlasting life I have because Jesus died for me sins. But the *feelin's* all gone, Son!"

Patrick ran for the Bible. Hurrying to find John 3:36, he shouted, "Mother, Mother, it's still in the book. Sure enough! And Mother doesn't it say as plain as your nose, 'He that believeth on the Son *hath* everlasting life.' "

"Oh, Son, it's that happy I am, that it's in God's book. Not me feelin's but what God says is what counts. Praise His name!"

God said it. Jesus did it. I believe it. that settles it.

Day 10   Read Ephesians 1:12, 13

Hide and Seek Words ☐
As you read your Bible try to find these hidden words:

"...sealed with that Holy Spirit"

For Always!

Tuck spent the summer on his uncle's ranch. He rode the range from morning to night. Oh what fun! One day he watched the horses being branded. He felt sorry to see the hot iron burn Uncle Ted's brand mark on their bodies. But the mark showed that the horses belonged to his uncle for keeps! They were his.

Suddenly it all became clear to Tuck—what it meant in the Bible about believers being sealed with the Holy Spirit until the day when Christ will return for us. We belong to Him forever! Although we can't see Him, we are marked by the Holy Spirit to show that God owns us.

I will seek to do God's will,
In all my work and play,
For I know that I shall go,
To live with Him some day.

Day 11   Read Ephesians 4:30-32

Hide and Seek Words ☐

As you read your Bible try to find these hidden words:

"...grieve not the Holy Spirit of God"

No Room for Sin

Heather found a dollar on the floor. She put the money in her pocket.

"I've lost a dollar and I can't find it anywhere," Mother said. But Heather said nothing. Soon she discovered she had lost that sweet feeling of peace which the Holy Spirit had put in her heart. It wasn't until she went to Mother and gave her the dollar that Heather had joy and peace again.

The Holy Spirit is the *holy* Spirit. He hates and despises sin. So must you if you want His friendship.

> Cleanse me from my sin, Lord,
> Put Your power within, Lord,
> Make my heart Your palace,
> And Your royal throne.

Day 12   Read John 15:5

Hide and Seek Words ☐

As you read your Bible try to find these hidden words:

"... without me ye can do nothing"

You Need Him!

After David decided to paint his floor, he rushed to the store, bought a bucket of paint and a brush, and started the job. Not until he was nearly through, did he discover that he had painted himself right into a corner! He had no way to get out!

Are you laughing at David? Wait a minute! Don't laugh too loud! For you are foolish when you try to plan your own life instead of asking God to plan it for you.

The Holy Spirit lives within you to be your *guide*. Ask Him to show you God's plan for you and for your whole life. Don't be like David and try to do things your own way!

Day 13   Read 1 Corinthians 6:19, 20

Hide and Seek Words

As you read your Bible try to find these hidden words:

"... ye are not your own"

Indian Chief Gives Indian Chief

"Indian Chief give his tomahawk to Jesus Christ," the Chief said.

Later he said, "Indian Chief give his blanket to Jesus Christ."

Again, he walked forward and said, "Indian Chief give his pony to Jesus Christ."

Then the Holy Spirit showed him that the Lord Jesus, who died for him, wanted the gift of *himself* more than anything else the chief could give. Then he said, "Indian Chief give himself to Jesus Christ."

The Holy Spirit says to each of us, "Give Me yourself!" Have you done it?

> Now, Lord, I give myself to You,
> I would be wholly Yours,
> Oh take me, seal me, for your own,
> Yours altogether, yours alone.
>
> —Havergal

Day 14   Read Romans 12:1

Hide and Seek Words ☐
As you read your Bible try to find these hidden words:

"... **present your bodies**"

I Did It!

A young boy sat in a church meeting. They were taking an offering of money to send the good news of salvation to other lands. When the baskets were brought forward and the money counted, a small white card was found. On the card three words were written—

I GIVE MYSELF

"Who put this in?" asked the preacher aloud. The young boy sitting in the back stood up and said, "I did. I give myself. It is all that I have to give." The boy had given more than any who gave money, for when he was grown he went to China as a missionary. Thousands of Chinese received the Lord Jesus because the missionary had given himself.

> Just as I am, young, strong and free,
> To let You live Your life through me;
> O Christ, I give my all to You,
> Lord of my life, I come, I come.

Day 15 — Read Romans 8:29

Hide and Seek Words ☐
As you read your Bible try to find these hidden words:

"... to be conformed [made like] ... his Son"

It Will Show!

God not only has a wonderful place for you in Heaven someday, He also has a special plan for your life on earth!

God's plan is that each day your life will become more like His. We know what God is like by the way His Son, the Lord Jesus, lived on earth. Can you really be like Him? Loving, kind, gentle, good? Only God could be like that. But wait a minute. Do you have God's life in you? Does God the Holy Spirit live in you? When you please God in all you do and say, others will be able to see that you aren't acting like *you* anymore. They will see God's life instead!

Day 16   Read Galatians 5:22, 23

Hide and Seek Words □

As you read your Bible try to find these hidden words:

"...the fruit of the Spirit is"

What Kind of Fruit?

In your verses God helps you understand what happens in your life when you obey His Spirit.

What kind of fruit do you see on an apple tree? Yes, the apples give *proof* that it is an apple tree. What kind of life should you see when you look at a Christian? A Christ-like life. God calls this life the "fruit" of the Spirit. When others can see your life is like Jesus' life, it is a *proof* that the Holy Spirit is living in you.

Look at your verses again. Find the nine things which are called the fruit of the Spirit. What kind of fruit do people see in your life?

Day 17 — Read John 15:26

Hide and Seek Words

As you read your Bible try to find these hidden words:

"... the Comforter is come"

He Understands

"Becky's mother died last week. When Becky came back to school today all she could do was put her head down on the desk and cry!"

"And what did you do?" Mother asked Rachel.

"Why, Mother, I just put my head down on the desk and cried with her."

When Jesus went back to Heaven, He promised to send us another Comforter in His place. That Comforter is the Holy Spirit. He helps you when you are sad. When He is in your heart you are able to comfort and show kindness to others as Rachel did.

"Comfort one another" (1 Thessalonians 4:18).

Day 18   Read 2 Corinthians 5:14, 15

Hide and Seek Words ☐
As you read your Bible try to find these hidden words:
"...live...unto him"

A Selfish Saint?

God has a new name for His children. He calls them *saints*. All those who receive the Lord Jesus as their Savior are saints. Sad to say, saints to not always act as they should! God keeps saying within, "Let Christ have His way in your heart!" Satan keeps telling you, "Do what I want you to! Be selfish; just think of yourself."

Let us who are saints be like the Holy Spirit. He does not speak of Himself, but of Christ (John 16:13, 14).

Day 19   Read Galatians 6:7-9

Hide and Seek Words ☐

As you read your Bible try to find these hidden words:

"... let us not be weary in well doing"

For Keeps!

"Waddle" was Jason's own special duck. Mr. Kind Neighbor had handed the duck to Jason and said, "He's all yours." Mr. Kind Neighbor came back many times to see how fast Waddle was growing, but he never took the duck back again! How *could* he? Didn't the duck now belong to Jason? Mr. Kind Neighbor didn't keep giving the duck to Jason over and over either. When he first gave him it was "for keeps."

Have you given yourself to God? Then you need not keep doing it over again. Just believe you are His. You have no right to take your life back again. You are to be *His for keeps.*

>   Jesus, my life is Yours
>   And evermore shall be
>   Hidden in You
>   For nothing can take
>   Your life from me.

Day 20   Read Acts 4:8-10

Hide and Seek Words ☐
As you read your Bible try to find these hidden words:

"...filled with the Holy Ghost"

How to Have Courage

Peter was a coward. He would not tell others he belonged to the Lord Jesus (Matthew 26:69-75). You and I are often cowards like this. Later Peter was very brave and spoke for the Lord with great courage. That is because he was *filled with the Holy Spirit*. God commands you too, to be filled with the Holy Spirit. Then you will not be ashamed to tell anyone of your Savior. How can you be filled with the Spirit? By obeying Him each day!

Scott and Roger were helping put up a tent where boys and girls could come and hear about the Lord Jesus. Friends from school came by and laughed at them! But the boys didn't care. They loved the Lord Jesus. They thanked God that they could be made fun of for Jesus' sake. They remembered He had even been willing to die for them!

Day 21 Read Romans 8:14, 15

Hide and Seek Words ☐

As you read your Bible try to find these hidden words:

"... led by the Spirit of God"

I Will Guide You

Penny was blind; but Penny had a guide. Pin Pin was her seeing-eye dog. All Penny needed to do was hold carefully to the rope and Pin Pin led her safely over the street crossings. He guided her to whatever place she needed to go.

You have a guide, too, and He is all-seeing. He is the Holy Spirit. One of the reasons Jesus sent Him to you is to guide you. He guides you as you study the Bible. He guides you as you listen to His quiet voice in your heart.

> Kept day by day in perfect peace
> His Spirit for my Guide;
> His Father mine, His Heaven my home,
> What do I need besides?

Day 22   Read 1 John 2:6

Hide and Seek Words ☐
As you read your Bible try to find these hidden words:

"... walk ... as he walked"

No More Temper!

Jeremy's job was only cleaning up dirty trash. But he didn't care! He wore a joyful smile because he was clean inside. He was cleansed by the blood of the Lord Jesus. Jeremy had one problem. He had a bad temper! At last, after he had failed many times, he asked the Lord to take over. He asked Him to fill his heart with the Holy Spirit. Jeremy found that as he let the Holy Spirit take charge of his life, he did not get angry at people. Jeremy wanted to live like Jesus would. Do you?

> Step by step, step by step
> I would walk with Jesus;
> All the day, all the way,
> Keeping step with Jesus.

Day 23   Read Ephesians 5:18

Hide and Seek Words ☐
As you read your Bible try to find these hidden words:

"... filled with the Spirit"

Someone Inside

"Mr. Carl," said Stephen to his camp leader, "when I am with you I do all right because you follow Christ. But when I am away from you I do all kinds of sin. You see, my folks aren't Christians, and it's sure hard to live for Christ at home."

"Stephen," Mr. Carl said, "suppose I could somehow get inside you and live your life for you. Do you think *that* would help?"

"Oh, that would be great, Mr. Carl, just what I need!"

"Well," answered Mr. Carl, "you have someone living in you who is mightier than I. He is God, the Holy Spirit. Trust Him to live His life in you, and you will do the right things!"

Fill me now, Lord Jesus,
Fill me as I pray,
Fill me with your Spirit,
Fill me every day.

—David H. Johnson

Day 24   Read 2 Timothy 1:6, 7

Hide and Seek Words ☐

As you read your Bible try to find these hidden words:

"...stir up [use] the gift of God"

Keep on Stirring

Elizabeth was making custard and she had to keep stirring it. If she didn't, it would stick and burn. It made her think of what she had heard at Bible club. The teacher told her that God gives each saved person a gift or *talent*. Some receive one gift and some another.

"Just to think," she said aloud, "that the children in many lands have never heard God's Word! Oh, how I want to go and be a missionary to them when I grow up. God wants some people to stay at home and pray, and some to give, but I believe He wants me to go. And if He does, I better be 'stirring up' the gift He has given me by telling the boys and girls right here how to be saved from sin!"

Day 25   Read 1 John 4:10-14

Hide and Seek Words ☐
As you read your Bible try to find these hidden words:

". . . we ought also to love"

A Bible Valentine

Tricia sat making her valentines. She didn't feel very wonderful inside, for she and Jennifer had quarreled. They said they would never speak to each other again as long as they lived! Tricia and Jennifer were both believers in the Lord Jesus. They had given their lives to the Lord. But they didn't act like it!

"Jennifer can just come to me first and make up; that's all!" Tricia pouted. Then the Holy Spirit brought a Bible verse to her mind which she had learned at Sunday school. She wrote it on a heart with paper lace around it. The next day Jennifer found it on her desk. How do you think she felt when she read the verse, "Beloved, if God so loved us, we ought also to love one another"? How do you think Tricia felt now?

Day 26   Read Romans 8:28

Hide and Seek Words ☐

As you read your Bible try to find these hidden words:

"... to them that love God"

God Works It Out

"I fell down and broke my leg," Johnnie said, "I was very unhappy to have to stay in during the summer while others were playing outdoors. But while I was in bed I learned to play my harmonica. Now I am leader of the harmonica band at school. God made even my broken leg work together for good!"

If you give your life to God, Romans 8:28 will be true for you. Even the things that seem the worst will turn out to be the very things God uses for the best. Don't forget that!

Day 27

Read Jude 20, 21

Hide and Seek Words ☐

As you read your Bible try to find these hidden words:

"...praying in the Holy Ghost"

The Spirit's Prayer

"I want you to meet my Joey," said a father to the preacher, as he held his lame son in his arms. "This is Joey. He led me to receive Christ. When the mission hall started, Joey said to me, 'Father, I can't go, but you can go with Mother and all the time you are gone I will pray.'"

"When I would get home, Joey would ask me, 'Did you come to Christ tonight, Father?' But last night he did not ask me. As the door opened and I lifted him up, he buried his face in my shoulder. He said, crying, 'You have believed on the Lord Jesus, I know you have!'"*

Joey had been praying *in the Spirit* for his father to be saved from his sin. When you pray in the Spirit, you do not just *say words*. The Holy Spirit helps you to know in your heart what you should pray for. God always answers prayers which are directed by the Holy Spirit.

*Adapted from J. Wilbur Chapman

Day 28   Read Hebrews 12:2

Hide and Seek Words ☐

As you read your Bible try to find these hidden words:

"... **looking unto Jesus**"

Look Up! Look Up!

One time a young boy found $5 on the street. After that he never looked up while walking. In several years this is what he found: 29,516 buttons, 54,172 pins, and 12 cents. He also received a bent back, and a grouchy look! He missed the blue sky, the song of birds, and the smile of friends.

If you belong to the Lord Jesus, don't be grumpy! Don't pout! Those who do not know the Savior have reason to be that way. But don't you be downhearted. You can always be happy when you look up to Jesus.

> Don't be downhearted, look up, look up!
> For Jesus is on His throne,
> And He will supply all your needs from on high,
> Cheer up! Cheer up! Cheer up!

Day 29   Read John 14:16, 17

Hide and Seek Words ☐

As you read your Bible try to find these hidden words:

"...he dwelleth with you and shall be in you"

God Cares!

Tippy was lonely. John, his master, had a new dog. John hung a sign around Tippy's neck which read: FOR SALE. John no longer wanted him. Tippy looked sad.

Sometimes you have that same lonely feeling that Tippy had. Your best friend has left you to be friends with someone else. But if you are a Christian you should not feel you have no friend! In the heart of every saved boy or girl lives the Stay-Within-Friend—the Holy Spirit. He is nearer and dearer than any other person. He is your companion and comforter. Remember that He is there no matter what!

You're not alone when skies are blue
God cares for you;
Even though there be both clouds and rain,
Or hours of pain,
His love shines through.

Day 30 Read Colossians 3:1, 2

Hide and Seek Words ☐
As you read your Bible try to find these hidden words:

"...your life is hid with Christ in God"

A Friend of God

Beth could not see, nor hear. She could not taste. She could not smell. A long fever had robbed her of all these senses which you have. But Miss Ellen had taught Beth to read from raised letters like blind people do. We call these letters Braille.

One day Miss Ellen heard Beth speaking when she went to her bedroom door, Beth was speaking to the Lord Jesus about the Bible verse which she had just spelled out with her fingers—"You are my friends if you do whatsoever I command you" (John 15:14). With her sightless eyes lifted to the Lord, Beth said, "Oh, I like to hear You say that! You only told me before that You were *my* Friend. I did not know that *I* am a friend of *Yours!*"

Beth was right! Isn't it wonderful that Jesus wants you for *His* friend! He is not only *in you*, but you are *in Him*. Your life is "hid with Christ in God."

Jesus Died for You and Me

Day 1   Read Genesis 3:8-10

Hide and Seek Words ☐

As you read your Bible try to find these hidden words:

"I was afraid... and I hid"

You Can't Hide

I watched a tiny boy the other day as he spread his chubby fingers in front of his face and thought he was hiding from his mother. How silly, you say. But sometimes older boys and girls, and even grown-up people, try to hide from God in this way! Do you remember how Adam and Eve tried to hide from God after they had sinned in the Garden? They were afraid, and hid themselves among the trees.

We cannot hide from God. God sees us. God knows all about us. And God loves us. He has provided a Savior, the Lord Jesus, to save us from our sins.

His Word tells us exactly what to do if we sin. Find 1 John 1:9 in your Bible and fill in the blank spaces: "If we_____ our sins, he is _____ and _____to forgive us our sins, and to cleanse us from all unrighteousness."

Day 2   Read Matthew 5:14-16

Hide and Seek Words ☐
As you read your Bible try to find these hidden words:
"Let your light . . . shine"

One Little Light

Long ago a young boy climbed with his father high up into a lighthouse to see the light. He knew that light shone seventy miles out to sea to warn sailors of danger and keep ships from crashing into the rocks. He expected to see a great big light. But he was surprised to find only one small kerosene lamp (it was before the days of electricity). The lighthouse keeper explained that by using prisms—clear glass cut into many sided figures to reflect the light—the tiny lamp's light was magnified a thousand times!

You say, "I'm just one little light. What can I do?" Read John 8:12 in your Bible. You can *reflect* the Light, and so shine for the Lord Jesus. Others seeing your light will find their way to Him who is the TRUE LIGHT!

"Jesus bids us shine with a clear, pure light,
Like a little candle burning in the night;
In this world of darkness we must shine
You in your small corner, and I in mine."

Day 3   Read John 6:5-11

Hide and Seek Words ☐

As you read your Bible try to find these hidden words:

"There is a lad here"

Three Important Things

Our Bible verses today tell of a young boy who was in the *right place,* had in his hand the *right things,* and in his heart a *right attitude.*

With a great crowd out on the grassy hillside, the boy listened to the wonderful things the Lord Jesus was telling. When supper time came, the lad willingly gave his five barley loaves and two fish to the Lord Jesus. The Lord Jesus used what the boy had to feed over five thousand people!

How about you? Are you willing for the Lord Jesus to use what you have so that others may hear about Him? Are you listening to His Word the Bible to learn His right place for you?

Think about the three important things. God can use you and make you a blessing to others as He did the lad we've read about.

1. right place
2. right things
3. right attitude

Day 4   Read Philippians 2:13

Hide and Seek Words ☐
As you read your Bible try to find these hidden words:
"God who worketh in you"

But I Hate Him!

"How can I love somebody I hate?" It was a hard question Allen asked his teacher at Sunday school.

"Really, Allen, you can't," the teacher replied, "but there is someone who can. The Lord Jesus who lives in you can do it. Tell Him you'd like to have Him love that person *through you*—using your mind and heart. He will."

"It worked! It worked!" Allen called excitedly to his teacher the next Sunday. "He was really nasty. But I said to the Lord Jesus: 'Okay, Lord Jesus. You live in me. You love him through me.' And all of a sudden, I didn't hate him anymore. And I feel so much better now."

The Lord Jesus can love others through you today. Trust Him to do it.

Day 5   Read Acts 5:27-32

Hide and Seek Words ☐
As you read your Bible try to find these hidden words:
"We ought to"

Is *Stubborn* Good or Bad?

We all know what *bad stubborn* is—not doing what we are told, not listening to others, getting our own way no matter what. But did you know there is *good stubborn* too?

This word *stubborn* is interesting. It comes from the word *stub*, which is a short stump of a tree from which all the branches are gone. The wind cannot move it. It stands firm, almost like a rock.

Good stubborn is like that. In our Bible verses for today, Peter said to the high priest who told him he could not tell others about the Lord Jesus, "We ought to obey God...." Peter said, "No matter what you do to us," he said, "we will obey God."

Are you *good stubborn*? Do you stand for the Lord Jesus even when your friends make fun of you? Do you refuse to take part in things that you know are wrong? Do you say, "I will obey God"?

Day 6 Read Luke 10:38-42

Hide and Seek Words ☐
As you read your Bible try to find these hidden words:

"But one thing is needful"

Sit and Listen

We all like to have special friends. The Lord Jesus had special friends He loved to visit while He was on the earth.

One home He loved to go to was that of Mary, Martha and their brother Lazarus. One evening after the Lord Jesus had preached and healed many people, He came to their home in Bethany. They must have known He was coming. Martha was busy making a big supper.

When the Lord Jesus sat down, Mary came and sat down at His feet and listened to His words. The Lord Jesus was pleased that Mary took time to *sit* and *listen*.

But Martha was upset. She thought Mary should be helping her with the supper. The Lord Jesus told Martha that Mary had chosen the good things to do.

Do you take time to sit and listen to His words? Read the verses from God's Word. Take time to talk to Him in prayer. Do you love Him most of all? The Lord Jesus says this is the *one thing* that is important.

Day 7   Read John 12:26

Hide and Seek Words ☐
As you read your Bible try to find these hidden words:

"... follow me"

Who Is Your Leader?

Did you ever hear of a *processional caterpillar?* These fuzzy little fellows follow each other in a line, each one following the caterpillar just ahead of him in a *parade.* One day a man watched these funny caterpillars as they marched around a large stone vase in his garden. He picked some of them up and put them in the gap between the first one and the last one so that there was a complete circle around the vase. Would you believe it, those caterpillars marched around that vase for a whole week!

Did you ever think about whom you are following? Do you do just what all of your friends do, even if it is wrong? Or are you brave enough to walk alone in order to obey the Lord Jesus?

Today, watch your step. Be sure you are walking in the right places, doing the right things. God needs leaders. He needs *you.*

Day 8   Read Matthew 4:18-20

Hide and Seek Words □

As you read your Bible try to find these hidden words:

"Follow me"

Follow the Leader

Did you ever play *Follow the Leader?* Everyone in the line is supposed to do exactly what the leader does. It is the most fun when the leader does something especially hard!

One day as Peter and his brother Andrew were fishing on the shore of the Sea of Galilee, the Lord Jesus came by and called to them, "Follow me...." The Lord Jesus wanted to be their leader. He wanted them to follow Him and be His disciples. And the Bible says *right away* they followed the Lord Jesus. They left their nets and their fish and followed Him, becoming His helpers.

The Lord Jesus calls you to be His follower, He has a plan for your life. He will never ask you to do anything *too hard*. He will help you to obey His Word. He will make you a happy follower.

Day 9   Read 1 John 1:9

Hide and Seek Words ☐

As you read your Bible try to find these hidden words:

"If we confess"

Confess It

I like Peter, one of Jesus' twelve disciples. Maybe it's because I'm like him. Peter was always getting into trouble because of his quick tongue. He was always sorry when he had done wrong. Read about him in Luke 22:54-62.

When the Lord Jesus was on trial, Peter was standing far off. Guess whom he was with—the enemies of the Lord Jesus! When they asked him about Jesus, Peter said he didn't even know Him. Then Peter swore!

Later the Lord Jesus passed close to Peter as He was led away to be crucified. He looked right into Peter's eyes. Peter just ran away and cried, he was so sorry for what he had done. But that's the reason the Lord Jesus died—for Peter's sins and yours and mine!

Sometimes, like Peter, do you forget to let the Lord control your life? Do you allow sin to keep you from enjoying the Lord Jesus? He will forgive your sin if you *confess* or *tell* Him about the thing which you have done.

Day 10   Read Romans 1:16

Hide and Seek Words ☐

As you read your Bible try to find these hidden words:

"... the gospel of Christ"

What Is a Missionary?

Did you ever go on an errand for your mother? Perhaps she had an important message for someone and she asked you to take it. Or maybe she wrote a note and asked you to take it to the one she wanted to read it.

What is a missionary? The Bible tells us that *a missionary is one who is sent with a message.* He is to take the good news of the Gospel to those who need to hear. The Lord Jesus died to save us from our sins; He rose again and lives in Heaven for us. Surely *that* is good news!

We read in God's Word that we are His messengers. Have you received the Lord Jesus as your Savior from sin? Then you are a missionary.

Let's read our verse again. Was the Apostle Paul ashamed of the message he was to give? Are you ashamed to let others know what the Lord Jesus has done for you? Be a missionary—share the message with someone today.

Day 11　　　　　　　　　　Read Psalm 9:1, 2

Hide and Seek Words ☐
As you read your Bible try to find these hidden words:

"... with my whole heart"

Where Is a Missionary?

On the way home, after hearing a missionary speak, Jim said to his mother, "I think I would like to be a missionary someday." His wise mother said, "Jim, you are a missionary *right now!*"

"But I thought a missionary had to go to another country," said Jim.

When they arrived home, Jim's mother drew him a picture. On the paper she put a small circle. "God has given you this little circle in which to live for Him and love Him with all your heart."

"Probably that means right here at home," said Jim.

Mother drew a large circle around the small one.

"God will give you a larger circle when you fill the small one."

"I'm going to be faithful in my small circle and maybe someday God will give me a great big circle. Then I'll be ready to be a missionary in the big circle too!"

Day 12   Read Romans 10:14
_____

Hide and Seek Words ☐
As you read your Bible try to find these hidden words:

". . . how shall they hear?"

How About You?

Have you ever thought about what you want to be when you grow up? Of course you have! Perhaps if you are a girl you would like to be a teacher, or a nurse. Boys like to think about becoming a doctor, or a pilot of a plane, a radio operator, or a pastor.

God needs you, no matter what kind of work you do when you grow up. You might think, *I cannot work for God unless I am a pastor.* Oh, no! God needs pilots to fly missionary planes so that missionaries can get to their stations quicker, and so supplies can be taken to them. He needs doctors and nurses who are not afraid to tell others about His Son. He can even use radio operators in our own land and around the world.

You are not too young to begin thinking and planning for your future. God knows already what *He* wants you to be. As you trust and obey Him, He will show that plan to you!

Day 13 — Read Genesis 4:9

Hide and Seek Words ☐

As you read your Bible try to find these hidden words:

"Am I my brother's keeper?"

I Don't Care!

When Cain asked this question, "Am I my brother's keeper?" he was really saying to God. "It's none of my business. How am I supposed to know where he is, or what he is doing?" But in his heart Cain knew that he was his brother's keeper. He was responsible for what he had done to Abel. (You can read the whole story in Genesis 4.)

Does what we do or say make a difference to others? Can we honestly say, *I am not going to pay attention to anyone else. I will just take care of myself and let others do the same?*

If we truly love the Lord Jesus, having received Him as Savior from sin, we will want others to receive Him too. We will think of others, especially those of our own family. We will love them, pray for them, and tell them that the Lord Jesus loves them too! Read the words of the Lord Jesus in John 13:34, 35.

Day 14   Read John 1:37-42

Hide and Seek Words ☐
As you read your Bible try to find these hidden words:
"He first findeth his own brother"

Come with Me

Let me tell you about a young man who *did* feel that he was his brother's keeper. Andrew and his friend John met the Lord Jesus one day, and they heard John the Baptist say, "Behold [see] the Lamb of God!"

They listened as the Lord Jesus spoke. They believed His words. They followed Him to the place where He was staying.

"I must go find my brother Peter," Andrew said. "I want him to know the Lord Jesus too." Andrew hurried away, found his brother and brought him to Jesus. Peter listened and believed the words of the Lord Jesus too! Peter, Andrew and John became disciples or followers of the Lord Jesus.

Later God used Peter to write two of the books of the New Testament. He also used him to win thousands of men, women, boys and girls to the Lord Jesus. Suppose Andrew had not brought Peter to the Lord Jesus.

Do you think God wants *you* to bring your family to the Lord Jesus?

Day 15   Read John 1:43-46

Hide and Seek Words ☐

As you read your Bible try to find these hidden words:

"Come and see"

Invite Your Friends

One day the Lord Jesus called Philip to be one of His disciples. How happy this must have made Philip. I am sure he wanted to tell all his friends about the Lord Jesus. One day Philip saw his friend Nathanael. "I have found the Christ," Philip said, "the one the Old Testament tells us would come to be the Savior of the whole world. He is Jesus of Nazareth."

Nathanael just couldn't believe such a great person would come from the town of Nazareth.

"Come and see for yourself," invited Philip. "Let Him talk to you as He talked to me. He will forgive your sins. He will make you clean and pure."

How glad Nathanael was that Philip told him about the Savior.

Did you ever think how glad *your* friends would be if you introduced them to the Lord Jesus Christ? Have you ever spoken to *one* friend about Jesus? Do it today!

Day 16　　　　　　　　　　Read Mark 5:19

Hide and Seek Words ☐
As you read your Bible try to find these hidden words:
"Go . . . and tell"

Turn About Face!

The Bible tells about a man who was in deep trouble. He was wild, and lived away from his family and friends. Men tried to chain him down because they were afraid of him, but he broke loose. Then one day the Lord Jesus Christ came to him and everything was changed. The Lord Jesus cleansed the man from his sins and healed his sick mind. How the man loved the Lord Jesus. How happy he was.

"Let me go with you always," the man begged the Lord Jesus.

"Go home to your friends," answered the Lord Jesus, "tell them how great things the Lord hath done for thee."

The man obeyed. Can't you imagine how amazed everyone was to see the great change in his life? I am sure many people believed in the Lord Jesus as Savior from sin because of this man.

The Lord Jesus has great power to change lives. Has He changed your life? Read 2 Corinthians 5:17.

Day 17   Read Acts 26:19

Hide and Seek Words ☐
As you read your Bible try to find these hidden words:
"... **not disobedient**"

He Obeyed

Our friend, Paul, learned to obey God. During the first part of his life he had disobeyed God. He was mean to the Christians, putting them in prison, perhaps even killing them. Then one day God spoke to Paul. A great light came from Heaven and blinded him. That day Paul understood that the Lord Jesus was truly the Son of God and received Him as his Savior from sin. From that time on Paul wanted to obey the Lord Jesus. He worked hard. He became a great missionary. He told people everywhere how the Lord Jesus could take away their sins and make them obedient people. Paul said about himself, "I was not disobedient to the heavenly vision."

Are you learning to obey God in everything? Are you careful to obey your parents? Perhaps God may call you to be a missionary for Him. Would you like that?

Day 18   Read Acts 9:15

Hide and Seek Words ☐

As you read your Bible try to find these hidden words:

"He is a chosen vessel"

God Chose You

A vessel? What is it? A hollow object made to contain something.

Our Bible verse today tells us Paul was a chosen vessel. Paul had been made clean and ready for use when he believed Jesus Christ was the Son of God and received Him as His Savior from sin. The Lord Jesus had chosen Paul to be a vessel, to carry or *bear* some thing very special for Him. You find it in your verse—the name of the Lord Jesus Christ.

Paul was willing to be used of God. He became the greatest missionary that ever lived. He wrote many of the books of the Bible. He traveled much telling everyone about the Lord Jesus the Savior of the world.

You are a chosen vessel too! The Lord Jesus wants to use you. Will you be a vessel to bear His name today? Use your voice to speak of His great love. Let your actions show you love Him.

Day 19   Read Philippians 3:14

Hide and Seek Words □
As you read your Bible try to find these hidden words:
"...for the prize"

God Has a Prize

The apostle Paul made up his mind he was going to do what God wanted him to do in everything.

Sometimes Paul had to suffer. He was put in prison. He was stoned. He went without food. He was shipwrecked. He was cold. He didn't have enough clothes to wear! But he pressed on, working hard.

He knew that in Heaven he would be rewarded! He didn't expect doing things for God to be easy. He said living for the Lord Jesus Christ and serving Him was like a race. He was running hard, according to God's rules, in order to win the prize! Read 1 Corinthians 9:24.

Day 20　　　　　　　　　　Read Philippians 4:4

Hide and Seek Words ☐

As you read your Bible try to find these hidden words:

"Rejoice"

It's Catching!

"What's for breakfast?" Jon called out cheerily as he took two steps at a time down the stairs toward the kitchen. Jon was always cheerful.

"It's just fun to have him around," his mother said to her friend. "He cheers up the rest of the family!"

Being happy is like that. You make other people happy too. It's catching!

There was a secret to Jon's cheerfulness. Every day when he opened his eyes—almost while he was still yawning—he would say: "God, You know I can't run my life. When I try, I always get into trouble. Will You run it for me?"

Sometimes Jon would forget and he would clobber some fellow who got in his way at school. He would have to say to the fellow "I'm sorry." Then he'd say to God—"I took over. Please forgive me." As soon as he had confessed his sin and asked God to take control again, Jon knew everything was all right, and he started singing...and cheering people up.

Day 21   Read Acts 5:29

Hide and Seek Words ☐
As you read your Bible try to find these hidden words:
"We ought to obey God"

Hard to Obey

Did you ever wonder why it is so much harder to obey than it is to disobey?

Long, long ago the very first man on earth (you know his name—Adam) disobeyed God. He had every chance to obey God.

We disobey our parents. We disobey our teachers. We all have sinned. But that is only half the story the Bible tells. God sent the Lord Jesus from Heaven to earth to be born a baby, to grow up, and to die on the cross for your sins and mine. The Lord Jesus had always obeyed His Father. He loved us so much He was willing to take the punishment for our sins. Read Romans 5:19.

Have you ever thanked the Lord Jesus for dying for your sins? Have you received Him as your Savior?

If you have, you will want to obey Him. And let me tell you a secret. Obeying your parents is really a part of obeying our great God in Heaven (Colossians 3:20)!

Day 22　　　　　　　Read 2 Corinthians 9:6, 7

Hide and Seek Words ☐

As you read your Bible try to find these hidden words:

"God loveth a cheerful giver"

What Can I Give?

Every year Missy's grandfather sent her five dollars for her birthday. She looked forward to having this much money to spend as she pleased. On the Sunday following her birthday, a missionary spoke in Missy's church. He told about the needs of the children in Taiwan where he taught about the Lord Jesus. Missy thought about the five dollars tucked away in her treasure chest.

All the way home in the car Missy thought about the needy children and how her money could help them. *But it's my own,* she thought, *and I want to spend it for me.*

She went to her room and got out the nice green bill. "Dear Lord, make me *want* to give it to the missionary," she prayed.

As the family rode to church that evening, Missy asked, "Mother, may I give my birthday money to the missionary?"

Missy's heart was singing. She was happy she could give her very own money to help the children faraway.

Day 23 — Romans 5:6-8

Hide and Seek Words ☐

As you read your Bible try to find these hidden words:

"... some would even dare to die"

The Highest Honor

John and Betty Stam went to China to tell boys and girls, men and women about the Lord Jesus. Wicked men who didn't like what they were doing killed them. Mr. and Mrs. Stam became what we call *martyrs*. They died for Jesus' sake.

Christians in other lands have been killed because they told people about the Lord Jesus. In some lands there are laws which say you must not tell people about Him. And if you do, you may be put in prison. Or even killed!

Aren't you glad there is no law like that in your land? But laws can change. Some of us may have to die for telling others about the Lord Jesus. Dying for Him is a great honor. God will give those who die for Jesus' sake a crown of LIFE (Revelation 2:10).

Day 24   Read Daniel 1:8

Hide and Seek Words ☐
As you read your Bible try to find these hidden words:
"Daniel purposed..."

A Strong Backbone

What does it mean to have a purpose? It is something you intend to do *no matter what*.

Daniel was a boy with a purpose. Many hundreds of years ago the king of Babylon captured some bright young fellows who lived in the land of Israel. The king ordered them to eat his best food for he wanted them to be big and strong to serve him.

"I cannot eat food from the king's table," said Daniel. Didn't Daniel like to eat? Why did he say no? The king's food had been offered to idols, and Daniel loved and trusted the true God in Heaven. Daniel said, "No matter what happens to me, I will be true to God."

Daniel didn't wait to see what others would do. He decided for himself what was right and then did it. Some would say he had a strong backbone. Daniel became a great missionary in the land of Babylon.

Do you know what is right, and then do you do it? Read James 4:17.

Day 25   Read Acts 3:6-10

Hide and Seek Words □

As you read your Bible try to find these hidden words:

"...such as I have"

Better Than Money

Long ago in the city of Jerusalem a lame man was carried by his friends to the Beautiful Gate of the temple to beg. One day two of Jesus' disciples, Peter and John, came by. The lame man stretched out his hand. He hoped they would give him some money. Peter told him they didn't have any money. But Peter gave the man something much better than money. Through power God had given to him, Peter told the lame man to get up and walk. And he did!

You and I have something wonderful to give to others. We have God's Word. God's Word tells about the Lord Jesus who can forgive sin and make people ready to go to Heaven.

This news is better than money. Plan to share it with someone today.

Day 26   Read 1 John 4:9-11

Hide and Seek Words ☐
As you read your Bible try to find these hidden words:

"...we ought also to love one another"

Carry It with You!

Do you remember what happened to the lame man yesterday?

It reminds me of another true story. One day while walking down the street of his city, a great prince came upon a beggar who held out his hand for some money. The prince felt in his pockets, but not a single coin could he find.

"I have no money with me," he told the beggar, "but I take your hand, and I love you."

The beggar said, "Thank you, sir. Love is also a gift."

The love God gives us for others is a precious gift. Let us show by our kindness, even to the unlovely, that God's love is in our hearts. Do you carry God's love with you?

If any little word of mine
May make a life the brighter,
If any little song of mine
May make a heart the lighter,
God help me speak that little word,
And take my bit of singing,
And drop it in some lonely heart,
To set the echoes ringing!

Day 27 Read Isaiah 43:10

Hide and Seek Words ☐
As you read your Bible try to find these hidden words:

"Ye are my witnesses"

When Should You Start?

A witness is one who knows something special.

Long ago the country of Syria was at war with Israel. Among those taken as prisoners of war was a young Israelite girl (little maid). She became a servant in the home of Naaman, a great general. Read about her in 2 Kings 5:1-3.

One day she learned her master had leprosy. She knew something special—the prophet of God in her country could make him well. But she was only a servant and so young. Should she be a witness and tell her master? Yes, she knew what God wanted her to do. And she did it.

Naaman heard the good news and believed the words of his young servant.

Are you a witness for God? Start today telling others of Him.

Day 28   Read Colossians 3:15-17

Hide and Seek Words ☐

As you read your Bible try to find these hidden words:

"Be ye thankful"

Want to Be Happy?

Does your mother ever have to remind you to say "please" or "thank you"? It is easy to forget, isn't it? It is important to say thank you with your lips. But it is far more important to say thank you with your heart.

What does it mean to say thank you with your heart? I think it means just making the best of the things you have, being glad you have them. It means thinking about the things God wants you to be thinking about and praising Him (Philippians 4:8). It means looking on the bright side, not grumbling or complaining. It means trying to make someone else happy because of the good things you have.

The more you are thankful, the more you will have to be thankful about. A thankful heart will make you a happy person. A bigger reason for being thankful is that you will make other people happy.

Most important of all, God loves to have you thank Him. How many things do you have to thank Him for right this minute?

Day 29   Read 1 Thessalonians 5:18

Hide and Seek Words ☐
As you read your Bible try to find these hidden words:

"In everything give thanks"

Be Thankful

One of God's great missionaries was John G. Paton, who lived for many years on the New Hebrides islands now called Vanuatu islands. At one time there was no food, and the people were very hungry. They watched every day for the missionary ship to come bring food. A large group of boys and girls were on the shore when the ship came for Mr. Paton had promised each of them a biscuit as soon as the food was unpacked.

As he gave each child a biscuit, he waited for them to eat it quickly for he knew how hungry they were. "Why don't you eat?" he asked.

"We shall first thank God for sending us food and ask Him to bless us all," one of them said.

If you were hungry, do you think you would wait to thank the Lord before eating?

Do you remember what the rest of today's Bible verse says?

Day 30   Read 2 Timothy 2:2

Hide and Seek Words □

As you read your Bible try to find these hidden words:

"...teach others also"

Others Waiting

John Paton worked hard to write the Bible in the language of the people of New Hebrides, now called Vanuatu. John knew the people needed to be able to read God's Word for themselves.

Every day the villagers questioned, "Is it finished?"

How happy John was the day he could tell them, "Yes!" He read God's Word to them. Shouting with joy, the chief cried, "It speaks like I speak." John taught the chief to read. And soon the chief was teaching others!

Do you remember about the circles? (Turn back to Day 11 if you've forgotten.) John Paton was faithful in his little circle, so God gave him a bigger work to do. And the circle continued to grow larger as the chief taught others.

Will you let God use you? Others are still waiting to hear about the Lord Jesus.

God's Word Is Really Powerful!

Day 1   Read 2 Timothy 3:16

Hide and Seek Words ☐

As you read your Bible try to find these hidden words:

"All Scripture is given by inspiration of God"

"Special Delivery"

Boys and girls like to know how things happen. Did you ever wonder where the Bible came from and how the people knew what to write? Your Hide and Seek words tell you! All Scripture (that means every part of the Bible) was given by God. Inspiration (in-spear-a-shun) means that God told the writers in their minds what to say. You might call it "Special Delivery" from God's mind to theirs!

Why did God give His words to us? The second part of your verse can be said this way: "The Bible teaches us what is true and makes us know what is right and what is wrong in our lives. If we obey the Bible, it will help us do what is right."

God wanted you to know these things because He loves you and wants you to be happy.

    I believe the Bible
        I believe the Bible
            I believe the Bible
IS THE WORD OF GOD!

Day 2   Read 2 Peter 1:20-21

Hide and Seek Words ☐

As you read your Bible try to find these hidden words:

"... they were moved by the Holy Ghost [Holy Spirit]"

Straight from Heaven

No part of the Bible was thought up by the men who wrote it down. God wants you to know that this Book is all HIS Book!

God did not use just anyone to write down His words. He used *holy* men—men who wanted to do what pleased God. They were moved or guided by God the Holy Spirit. He gave them the right words and ideas to write.

Since God used holy men to write His message and the Holy Spirit told them what to say, you can be sure that the Bible is straight from Heaven!

Stacey learned that the Bible is God's Word. She wanted to have a Quiet Time every day so that she would be sure to know what He had to say to her. But... she did not have a Bible of her own. Stacey went to her grandmother's house to borrow a Bible!

Holy men of old
Wrote what they were told.
'Twas given by God's Spirit,
So you and I could hear it.

Day 3   Read Romans 1:16

Hide and Seek Words ☐
As you read your Bible try to find these hidden words:

"...it is the power of God unto salvation"

Power to Save

Paul, one of God's greatest missionaries, wrote this verse. He was not ashamed of the Gospel (the good news) of Christ, because it has power to save us from sin!

Without God's Word, the Bible, you would never know that you are a sinner (that you do wrong things). Without God's Word you would not know that the Lord Jesus took the punishment for your sin. And you would not know that by believing He died for you, your sins are forgiven. Yes, God's Word is powerful.

Becky had learned a verse to recite at Sunday school—"Suffer the little children to come unto me and forbid them not" (Mark 10:14). But she got only as far as "Suffer the little children" after trying three times. Finally, Becky said, "Jesus wants us all to come to Him; and don't anybody try to stop us!" That is really what God meant! Have you ever told Him you believe Jesus died for you?

Day 4   Read Psalm 119:160

Hide and Seek Words □
As you read your Bible try to find these hidden words:

"...endureth for ever"

An Angry King

In Old Testament days King Jehoiakim didn't like God's words, so he burned the paper on which they were written! But God helped His messenger make a new copy of His commands to the king. God's Word endures (lasts) forever!

All through the years men have tried to destroy the Bible. Sometimes they tore it up. Sometimes it was burned. But God did not allow all copies to be destroyed. He knows that we need His words to tell us how to be right with Him.

Some years ago an important lawyer offered a reward of $1,000 to anyone who could find something untrue in the Bible. A number of people went to him and told him they found some mistakes. The lawyer knew better! He refused to pay, and so was taken before a judge. In the courtroom the people who said there were mistakes in the Bible could not prove even one of them. They had to leave the court—very embarrassed!

Day 5   Read Psalm 119:138

Hide and Seek Words ☐
As you read your Bible try to find these hidden words:
"Thy testimonies... are very faithful"
You Can Count On It!

"Testimonies" is another name for God's words. God tells us that His testimonies are faithful or true. You can count on the Bible!

God told us over 3,000 years ago (Job 38:7) that "the morning stars sing together." Today scientists with their strong instruments can hear sounds coming from stars!

Until the telescope was invented, people guessed that there were about 1,000 stars. Now you will learn in school that there are so many stars they cannot be counted. But what was written in the Bible thousands of years before telescopes were invented? God told us that the stars are as many as the sand upon the seashore! (Genesis 22:17)

The wonderful thing is that as you read God's Word and ask Him to help you, you can become faithful. God will be able to count on you!

> God's Word is very faithful.
> It will guide in all I do.
> As I read it every day,
> I will be faithful, too.

Day 6   Read Psalm 119:89-90

Hide and Seek Words ☐
As you read your Bible try to find these hidden words:
"... thy word is settled in heaven"

That Settles It!

Do you know what the very middle verse of the Bible is? It says something like this: "It is better to trust [or believe] in the Lord than to put your trust in man" (Psalm 118:8).

Some boys and girls listen only to what *people* say. Your Hide and Seek Words today tell you why it is better to believe the Lord. "Thy word is settled in heaven" means that the Bible is *always* true. God said it and that settles it!

People here on earth change their minds. Some men once thought that the earth rested on the shoulders of a huge invisible elephant! Now that men understand more about the earth and space, they know better.

But God told us in the Old Testament (Job 26:7) that *He* "hangeth the earth upon nothing!" He knows all things from beginning to end. His Word never changes.

If someone says something different than God says, whom will you believe?

Day 7 — Read Psalm 33:6

Hide and Seek Words ☐

As you read your Bible try to find these hidden words:

"By the word of the Lord were the heavens made"

Powerful Words

Spaceships, astronauts, moon missions. How exciting! Did you ever stop to think of all the thousands and thousands of dollars needed to get just *one* rocket into space? And what about all the hundreds of hours men have worked to get ready for "blast off"? Man works very hard for his power.

Do you remember how God made the world? He just *said* "Let there be light" and there was light. He *said* "Let the earth bring forth animals" and it happened! "By the word of the Lord were the heavens made." God's words have great power.

As you read the Bible each day, His words will come into your mind. Believe what He says with all your heart. Then you will have power to do even the hardest things in your life.

Day 8   Read John 5:24

Hide and Seek Words ☐
As you read your Bible try to find these hidden words:
"He...hath [has] everlasting life"

Nothing to Cry About

"Mother, don't cry, please. It's all right. I know that when I die I am going to Heaven to be with the Lord Jesus." Andy was nine years old and very sick. The doctors told his mother he would not get well.

Andy had asked Jesus to be his Savior from sin. He knew he was now God's child and he wasn't afraid. Andy knew he would go to Heaven when he died. He knew a promise in God's Word which told him so.

Do you know that promise?

Jesus said, "In my Father's house are many mansions...I go to prepare a place for you...that where I am there you may be also" (John 14:2, 3).

By believing God's Word, you can *know* you have everlasting life—the kind of life you need to live in Heaven someday. If you have believed in the Lord Jesus as your Savior from sin, you need never be afraid to die.

Day 9 — Read Mark 5:41, 42

Hide and Seek Words

As you read your Bible try to find these hidden words:

"I [Jesus] say unto thee arise"

It's a Miracle

"It's a miracle! It's a miracle!" Can't you just hear the people after the Lord Jesus spoke and the girl got up—all well again? For anyone else to make this girl live again would have been impossible, but for God nothing is impossible.

A miracle happens when you ask the Lord Jesus to forgive your sin and to live in your heart. It is a miracle when God changes your sinful heart so that you want to obey Him. You receive new life from God, and are born into His family.

Here are five important things to help you remember how to be born into God's family:

God loves me.
I have sinned.
Christ died for me.
I receive Him.
I am saved.

Day 10   Read Mark 10:51, 52

Hide and Seek Words ☐

As you read your Bible try to find these hidden words:

"Immediately he received his sight"

Darkness or Light?

"I can't see! I can't see!" Beth cried. A storm had caused the electricity to go off. The house was dark and Beth was afraid. The moment the lights were on again Beth stopped crying.

God tells you that if you have not asked the Lord Jesus to forgive your sins, you cannot see Him. Your sins separate you from God. It is like being in the dark.

In your Bible verses can you find two things that the blind man did to receive his sight?* This is the same way you can have the darkness of sin taken away. Ask Jesus to forgive your sin and believe He will do it. If you have never done this, do it now! If you have already believed on the Lord Jesus, He says you are living in the light. Thank Him today.

"Once I was blind, but now I can see.

   The light of the world is Jesus."

*He *asked* to see
and he *believed*
that Jesus could give him sight.

Day 11   Read Luke 7:6, 7

Hide and Seek Words ☐

As you read your Bible try to find these hidden words:

"Say in a word, and my servant shall be healed"

No Other Way

"Daddy, let me come down and help you," Ann called to her father as she stood above the trap door to the basement. Her father had gotten down by a ladder that was now being used in another part of the basement.

Ann's father walked to the opening and said, "Jump, and I'll catch you."

It was dark and Ann could hardly see her father. "No, no. I'm afraid," she called down.

"Ann, trust me! You know Daddy will catch you." And he did!

Ann needed to believe her father's words. Just so God wants you to trust His words. How sad it makes Him when you are afraid instead of believing He loves and cares for you.

"Trust and obey,
For there's no other way
to be happy in Jesus,
but to trust and obey."

Day 12   Read Matthew 8:25-27

Hide and Seek Words ☐
As you read your Bible try to find these hidden words:

"Even the wind and the sea obey him"

He's in Control

In the Old Testament you can read about a very great fish, under very special orders. God told the fish to swim to a ship. Because he had disobeyed, God's servant, Jonah, was to be thrown overboard. The great fish was ordered to swallow Jonah. God kept him safe inside the fish.

At another time God told hungry lions His servant Daniel would be thrown into their den, but they were not to touch him. They did exactly as they were told.

God is in control of weather, animals, people...everything. You can trust Him in whatever need you have today. Tell Him about it right now. He will care for you. He's in control.

Day 13   Read Matthew 4:18, 19

Hide and Seek Words ☐

As you read your Bible try to find these hidden words:

"Follow me"

Will You Answer?

Smiling from ear to ear, Ricky visited a *Good News Club*™ in Brazil. After the club was over, he did not leave. He looked very serious. "What is wrong?" the teacher asked.

Ricky said, "I knew Jesus died, but I never knew He died for *me*!"

The teacher showed him verses in God's Word which helped him understand. Ricky believed on the Lord Jesus as his very own Savior from sin. With tears in his eyes, he said, "When I get to Heaven, I want to be the first one to stand before Jesus and thank Him!"

While the Lord Jesus was here on earth He called people to follow Him—Matthew, Peter, John, Andrew and many others. If you have believed on the Lord Jesus, He calls *you* to follow Him. Will you answer "yes"? To follow Jesus is *to decide to please Him above anyone else.*

Day 14   Read Micah 5:2; Luke 2:11

Hide and Seek Words ☐
As you read your Bible try to find these hidden words:
"In the city of David [Bethlehem]"

Telling the Future

A prophecy (prof-e-see) is *something that God tells before it happens.*

When Adam and Eve disobeyed God and had to leave the garden, God promised that one day a Savior would come who would die for the sins of all people.

Hundreds of years passed. Many of the men whom God used to write our Old Testament wrote about the one who was to come. Each thing that God told them about His Son was a prophecy.

Micah was one of the men who wrote down God's Word. He wrote that the Savior would be born in Bethlehem—over 700 years before it happened! Can you imagine how excited the shepherds were that night when the angel said the Savior had finally come? No wonder they went to find Him right away. God had kept His promise!

In the Bible are hundreds of prophecies which have come true. This is one way we know it is God's Word.

Day 15   Read John 4:25, 26

Hide and Seek Words ☐

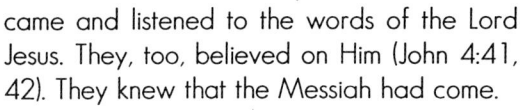

As you read your Bible try to find these hidden words:

"I know that Messias [the promised Savior] cometh"

He Has Come

The Lord Jesus talked one day with a woman who came to a well where He sat. She had done many wrong things and was very unhappy. When the Lord Jesus told her He could give her *living water,* she didn't understand that He meant *everlasting life.* He also told this woman all about her past life. How surprised she was that He knew so much about her!

She told Jesus that when the Messiah came, the one who would save the people from sin, He would be able to tell them everything. Then Jesus told her *He* was the Messiah. He was the prophecy come true!

The woman believed on the Lord Jesus. She went at once to tell her friends. They came and listened to the words of the Lord Jesus. They, too, believed on Him (John 4:41, 42). They knew that the Messiah had come.

Day 16 Read Isaiah 53:6; John 10:11

Hide and Seek Words ☐
As you read your Bible try to find these hidden words:

"... the iniquity of us all"

It Is Finished

While the Lord Jesus was here on earth He often told His disciples that He would die. It was hard for them to believe. They even offered to stand by Him if others tried to harm Him. But Jesus wanted them to understand that He came to earth for that very reason—to die for the sins of all people.

Isaiah wrote down a prophecy from God, long before the Savior came. It was that God the Father would put all the sins of everyone in the world on the Lord Jesus. He Himself would take the punishment that should have been ours (Isaiah 53:6).

The Lord Jesus cried out from the cross before He died, "It is finished." He meant that He had done what God sent Him to do. He had paid for our sins with His own life's blood.

All the prophecies about a promised Savior came true in the Lord Jesus. God's own Son is the Savior of the world. He died for you!

Day 17 Read Luke 24:25-27

Hide and Seek Words ☐
As you read your Bible try to find these hidden words:
"Believe all that the prophets have spoken"

A Surprise Visitor

In your verses today the Lord Jesus is talking to two friends who were walking to Emmaus. They were very sad. They didn't even know the Lord Jesus when He came and walked with them. They told Him why they were sad—the one they thought would be the Savior was dead!

Jesus told them many things that the Old Testament prophesied about Him. In the books written by Moses, in the Psalms, and in the books written by the prophets, it was told that the Savior would come to earth, die, and rise again from the dead!

At last the two friends knew who was talking with them—Jesus Himself! They had not expected to see Him alive again. They hurried all the way back to Jerusalem to tell His disciples this good news.

Day 18　　　　　　　　　Read Acts 1:10, 11

Hide and Seek Words ☐
As you read your Bible try to find these hidden words:
"This same Jesus... shall so come"

He's Coming!

Forty days after the Lord Jesus rose from the grave, He was with His disciples on the Mount of Olives. Suddenly, right before their eyes, they saw Him going up in the clouds into Heaven.

Two of God's messengers came and told the disciples the Lord Jesus would return in the same way He had gone away. This was another prophecy.

All that the Old Testament writers had said would happen did happen. Just as those words came true, so will the prophecy of His return. We do not know *when* He will come, but we know He will!

If you were expecting an important guest at your house, you would want everything to be ready, wouldn't you? Just so, we need to keep our lives pure each day as we look for the coming of our Savior. Read 1 John 3:3.

Day 19   Read Amos 9:14, 15

Hide and Seek Words □
As you read your Bible try to find these hidden words:

"They shall no more be pulled out of their land"

No Fooling!

What special group of people did God first choose to tell the world about Him?* But when they did not obey Him, they had to be punished. God let enemies take over their country. The Jewish people had to move to all parts of the world.

God told His people over 2,000 years ago to look for something good to happen in the *future*. Amos wrote it in the verses you read today. God promised that He would bring the Jews back to their land again.

The Jewish people have their special land in Israel now. Each year more and more of them are going there to live. We can see God's prophecy coming true!

"What is faith?" the teacher asked. Steve had a good answer, "It means to believe that God isn't fooling. You can believe God really means what He says!"

*The Jews

Day 20   Read 2 Timothy 4:4

Hide and Seek Words ☐
As you read your Bible try to find these hidden words:

"...they shall turn away ...from the truth"

Lies from Satan

God tells us in His book the Bible that He made us like Himself. People have made up a fable (a lie) that we have come from monkeys! Some people even say they believe God is dead.

Why do people believe lies instead of believing God? It is because of sin. God's enemy Satan puts these thoughts in their minds. God's prophecy is coming true—people are turning away from the truth and turning to lies.

Not believing God does not change His Word. It is still true. Some day all sin must be punished. If a person refuses to believe the Lord Jesus Christ, God's Son, took his punishment for sin, he will have to take the punishment for himself. "The wages of sin is death [separation from God] but the gift of God is eternal life through Jesus Christ our Lord" (Romans 6:23).

Let's help others learn of God's gift.

Day 21   Read Hebrews 4:12

Hide and Seek Words ☐
As you read your Bible try to find these hidden words:
"The word of God is ... a discerner ... of the heart"

Powerful! Sharp! Piercing!

So far in this booklet you have learned where the Bible came from, how powerful God's Word is, and that it tells the future. On the rest of the pages you will find out that God's Word has power to do things for YOU!

A sword is a weapon that can easily cut into something. It is powerful. But God's Word is more powerful than a sword!

When a sinner reads the Bible, the words go right to his heart. They have power to show him he is a sinner and that he needs a Savior. God's Word is so powerful it can change the most wicked person into a child of God.

Are you a child of God? The Bible can show you the things in your heart and mind which are not pleasing to God. "The word of God is ... a discerner." This means it can point out what is good and what is bad in your life.

Day 22   Read Psalm 119:129, 130

Hide and Seek Words ☐

As you read your Bible try to find these hidden words:

"The entrance of thy words giveth light"

Light from Words

Masaki lived in a jungle village. One day he had a chance to visit the big city. When he returned home, his friends were excited to see what he had bought. "It's to keep me dry when it rains," Masaki explained proudly, as he showed them his first umbrella.

The rains came. All the children gathered to see if the umbrella really worked. Masaki walked out of his hut with the umbrella swinging on his arm! Of course, he got very wet, and everyone had a good laugh. Masaki did not know that he had to open the umbrella and hold it over his head if he wanted it to do its job.

Could it be that you are sometimes like Masaki? God has promised that if you let His words enter your heart and mind, they will be like a light. His words will show you more about Him and His plan for you. But you must open the Bible every day and read it, or it cannot do its job!

Day 23   Read John 8:31, 32

Hide and Seek Words □
As you read your Bible try to find these hidden words:
"The truth shall make you free"

Truly Free!

"I feel so free!" said a boy in California who had asked the Lord Jesus to be his Savior. "My cousin and I used to do bad things. I used to steal. But I don't want to do those things anymore. It's like a heavy burden rolled off my back."

Before we receive the Lord Jesus, we are like slaves. Sin is our master. But Jesus has no sin. He is filled with truth. When He comes into your heart and forgives your sin, He sets you free from its power. You no longer have to obey your old master!

Even though a Christian has power to say "NO" to sin, that old master does not give up. He keeps trying to get you to do wrong. God's Word helps you to be strong against sin. Here are some special promises to remember:

"Greater is he [Jesus] that is in you, than he [Satan] that is in the world" (1 John 4:4b).

"I can do all things through Christ who strengtheneth me" (Philippians 4:13).

Day 24 — Read Psalm 119:9-11

Hide and Seek Words ☐
As you read your Bible try to find these hidden words:

"Wherewithal [how shall] a young man cleanse his way?"

Pay Attention!

Now that Brian was a Christian he wanted to please God. But something was bothering him. "How do I know what God wants me to do?" he asked as he wrinkled up his forehead and looked very serious.

Check Psalm 119:9 again. Brian's question *and* answer are there. How can a boy or girl know what God wants him to do? By taking heed [paying attention] to the Word of God.

Yes, God tells us exactly what He wants us to do in His Word. In only two verses in Ephesians 4:31, 32, He tells us this:

> Don't be angry
> Don't speak evil
> Don't hate others
> Be kind to people
> Forgive anything

Search the Bible, pay attention to what it says and obey God.

Day 25   Read 2 Peter 3:18

Hide and Seek Words ☐
As you read your Bible try to find these hidden words:

"Grow . . . in the knowledge of our Lord and Savior"

Growing for God

Without God's gift of life no one's body can grow. The same is true in your *spiritual life* (the new life inside that you receive when you believe on the Lord Jesus). Your spiritual life grows only as you study and obey God's Word. If you refuse to grow God's way, you become a weak Christian.

It must make God feel very sad when He sees that some of His children are not growing up spiritually. Perhaps they still tell lies, or they do not love their enemies. It may be that some are selfish. Perhaps they are spending all their time doing things for themselves instead of telling others the way to Heaven.

Be sure that YOU read your Bible and pray every day. This will be like "food" and "exercise" to make your spiritual life strong. Then you will be ready when God asks you to do a job for Him!

I WANT TO BE A WORKER FOR THE LORD.

Day 26 Read Psalm 119:97, 98

Hide and Seek Words ☐

As you read your Bible try to find these hidden words:

"Thy commandments hast made me wiser than mine enemies"

How to Be Wise

As you think about Daniel today, you will see how the Hide and Seek words worked for him.

Daniel was taken to a strange land, among people who worshiped idols. Right away he decided in his heart he would obey the commandments of God—no matter what might happen to him!

God rewarded Daniel for his decision. He was able to live for God a long time, even though he was surrounded by wicked people. It never became easy for Daniel. He had enemies. But because Daniel obeyed God's commands, he was truly made *wiser than his enemies.*

The same God who was with Daniel is in control of our world today. God promises through His Word (His commandments) to give you wisdom—to help you stand up for Him even when the people around you do not.

Stand up, stand up for Jesus
Stand in His strength alone.

Day 27   Read Psalm 119:50

Hide and Seek Words ☐
As you read your Bible try to find these hidden words:

"This is my comfort ... thy Word"

Cheer Up!

Can you smile and be happy...
When something hurts?
when you are lonely?
when everything is going wrong?

Sickness and problems are sometimes called *afflictions*. Afflictions usually make you feel downhearted. That feeling causes the corners of your mouth to turn down and sometimes there are even tears.

CHEER UP! God has comfort (help) for you. Today's verse says that *His words* will quicken (cheer) you. Here are some of God's words that can make you feel better, no matter what the trouble is:

Jesus said, "My peace I give unto you... let not your heart be troubled, neither let it be afraid" (John 14:27).

"Casting all your care upon him [God], for he cares for you" (1 Peter 5:7).

Jesus said, "...I will never leave you nor forsake you..." (Hebrews 13:5).

Day 28   Read 2 Peter 1:4

Hide and Seek Words ☐
As you read your Bible try to find these hidden words:

"... partakers of the divine nature"

Becoming Like Jesus

Did you ever wonder why there are so many promises in the Bible? One reason is that God's children living in a sinful world need a lot of help and encouragement.

Your Bible verse gives another reason. God's great promises are given so that we might be "partakers of the divine nature"—so that we can become more like the Lord Jesus!

If you were to take a sponge and dip it in water, then squeeze it, what would come out? Orange juice? Milk? Of course not. Water would come out. If you look at bad pictures in magazines, watch awful stories on TV, read dirty books and listen to dirty jokes, all these things go into your mind. After a while what will come out of your life? Nice words? Kindness? Good deeds? No, the bad things you put in will come out.

Just so, if you put God's wonderful promises into your mind, you will become more like Him!

John 10:28; John 14:2; 3; Hebrews 13:5; Jeremiah 33:3

Day 29 — Read Romans 1:16

Hide and Seek Words

As you read your Bible try to find these hidden words:

"I am not ashamed of the gospel of Christ"

Something to Be Proud of!

The Gospel is the part of God's Word which says: Jesus died for our sins, was buried and rose again. The great missionary Paul said he was not ashamed to tell the Gospel because it has power to save those who believe it.

Mike saw the power of the Gospel one day. Here's how he tells what happened: "This boy lives next door and stole things—money, pills and stuff. I told him the Gospel—that Jesus loved him and had died for his sins. Then when it was time for camp, I went to his house again and asked him if he had received Jesus as his Savior yet. He asked how to do it. I told him. So right then he believed and was saved. And now he's stopped stealing!"

You need never be ashamed to tell a friend the Gospel. He may not receive Jesus right away. But because God's words have power, he will think about them. Maybe the next time you talk to him about Jesus, your friend will believe! The Gospel is something to be proud of.

Day 30 — Read Psalm 119:133

Hide and Seek Words

As you read your Bible try to find these hidden words:

"Order my steps in thy word"

God's Map

"Turn right on Route 322. Go seven miles, then go west on Route 23. Drive 10 more miles and we will be there!" Tim enjoyed giving the orders to his dad as he read the road map.

Every day of your life is like taking a trip. The things you decide to do are like steps on the journey of life. How wonderful it is that God has given you a "map" to tell you how to take these "steps." You guessed it! The *Bible* is God's map for your life.

As you get your orders from His Word, you can be sure that your life is going in the right direction. Iniquity (sin) will not have dominion (power) to lead you the wrong way.

God tells you in Psalm 119:105 that His Word is also like a *light* to show you the way to go. You do not have to worry about what is coming tomorrow.

Don't Be Sad, God Cares

Day 1   Read John 1:3

Hide and Seek Words ☐
As you read your Bible try to find these hidden words:

"All things were made by him"

God Loves His Creation

Have you ever thought about the great care God used when He created everything in this world? The ugly hippopotamus, who spends much time in the water, has his eyes, ears, and nostrils at the top of his head. He can see, hear, and smell an enemy coming and duck under the water. He can even close his ears and nostrils so the water won't go into them.

A plant, the Venus's-flytrap, has some wonderful perfume to attract insects and some juice to digest them. It needed some way to catch insects. God placed little triggers on the flower! When the insect hits the triggers, the flower snaps shut!

Every little flower that grows,
Every little grassy blade,
Every little dewdrop shows
Jesus' care for all He made
Jesus loves, and Jesus knows!
So you need not be afraid!

—Frances R. Havergal

Day 2   Read Matthew 20:34

Hide and Seek Words ☐

As you read your Bible try to find these hidden words:

"Jesus had compassion [sympathy] on them"

He Makes the Difference

Carol and Karen, the Bailey twins, usually did things together, even walking into the hospital, and—much later—walking out again—minus their tonsils. They both had very sore throats and ate lots of ice cream.

There was one big difference though. Carol was cheerful and uncomplaining, but Karen's face wore a frown. Many times she was in tears.

"How can you smile all the time?" asked Karen. "Your throat must not hurt."

But Carol answered, "Yes, it really does; but I know the Lord Jesus is especially with me right now."

"What makes you think that?" Karen questioned.

"Because while He was on earth, He showed a special love for those who were sick. He always took time for them, making them well. And I know He's with me, too."

Day 3   Read Matthew 5:16

Hide and Seek Words ☐
As you read your Bible try to find these hidden words:
"Let your light so shine before men"

Bright Lights

Some ladies of Costa Rica have some very unusual live "jewelry"—firebeetles. They catch these insects, attaching them to tiny chains or strings which the women wear around their waists, on their dresses, or in their hair. The glowing light from these firebeetles looks like sparkling jewelry fit for a queen.

If you have received the Lord Jesus, you should let your light shine so others may see Him. Your light is seen through the good things which you do. One way to let your light shine is to smile, even when things seem to go wrong.

I'll ask the Savior for His help
To smile and work and sing,
To keep the sunshine in my heart,
To help in everything.
And if I always please Him well
In what I say and do,
Then others may the Savior see
And want to please Him too.

Day 4   Read 2 Timothy 2:3

Hide and Seek Words ☐

As you read your Bible try to find these hidden words:

"Endure hardness, as a good soldier"

Soldiers

The night was dark—just what the soldier needed as he crept, sometimes on all fours, sometimes on his stomach, through this "no-man's-land." Cut off from the rest of the army, he must get the message through.

Suddenly the enemy saw his shadow and shouted an order. But the goal was near. He dashed beyond the reach of enemy guns. Panting and trembling with weariness, but tail wagging, he walked up to his master.

Yes, this was a K-9 soldier, a dog trained to carry messages. He had not given up but had finished his job.

We, too, are soldiers—Christian soldiers. It is not always easy to stand against the things that are wrong and do the right. But with the Lord Jesus as our Captain, we can be strong soldiers for Him.

Day 5   Read James 1:12

Hide and Seek Words ☐
As you read your Bible try to find these hidden words:
"He shall receive the crown of life"

Winning the Race

Danny was beginning to wonder if he could run much farther; he was so tired. He didn't think anyone was ahead of him in this race but he could hear at least one pair of feet running close by.

Then someone from the sidelines hollered, "Hey, Danny, want a drink of water?" And someone else called, "Your shoestring is untied, Danny."

He knew those voices belonged to the ones who wanted Mike to win. They were trying to distract him. But Danny didn't listen to them: he was out to win. And win he did!

We are in a race—the Christian race. Satan tries to distract—he tempts us to do wrong and to turn from God's way. In the Christian race, we must follow the Lord Jesus and His Word. The Lord Jesus has promised a crown (a prize) to those who love Him.

Day 6   Read Hebrews 13:6

Hide and Seek Words □

As you read your Bible try to find these hidden words:

"The Lord is my helper"

The Five-Finger Promise

"Mommy, I'm scared, I just know I'll forget my piece when I get up before all those people," Tanya cried.

"The Lord Jesus will help you, Honey," her mother said, "just like a verse in the Bible says, 'the Lord is my helper.' To help you remember, let's pretend to put one word on each finger of your right hand. We'll start with the little finger. That will put *my* on the pointer finger, and that is the one to hold on to. See, 'the Lord is *my* helper.'"

That night Tanya stood up and bravely said her piece so loud and clear. And anyone who was closely watching might have noticed her holding tightly to her pointer finger.

Thank the Lord Jesus that He is your helper. Place the Hide and Seek Words on your fingers to help you remember as Tanya did.

The Lord is my helper.

Day 7   Read Daniel 6:22

Hide and Seek Words ☐

As you read your Bible try to find these hidden words:

"My God ... sent his angel"

Heavenly Bodyguards

A big flock of chickens was feeding quietly when off to one side came a bad tempered turkey.

"I'll show those little chickens who's boss," he gobbled. "They better scatter and let me eat here."

He didn't make it to the first chicken though for 'wham-o'—something hit him. He turned to find who his enemy was only to discover that it was right on top of him. His feathers flew everywhere and he ran for his life. The trumpet bird, guardian of the flock, had won again.

God's children, too, have guardians or protectors. They are angels sent by God. Just think—an angel to watch over you at night, in school, at play, or wherever you are. Yes, private bodyguards. Isn't He a wonderful Heavenly Father? You are kept safe in His loving care.

Day 8   Read Galatians 6:9

Hide and Seek Words ☐

As you read your Bible try to find these hidden words:

"Let us not be weary [tired] in well doing"

Stick to It

In the ant kingdom there are groups of ants which have the most tiresome job I believe any insect could have. They are storage tanks. With the help of other ants, they fill their special stomach with a sweet juice which will be food for the ant colony in the seasons when they cannot get other food. So with stomachs about eight times the size they should be, the storage ants cling to the roof of their home with a lifetime job of bringing a drop of "honey dew" when one of their brothers or sisters wants it. Doesn't sound very exciting, does it?

Sometimes you, too, may have a job which does not seem very important or exciting. But if it is what God wants you to do, it is important to Him. And He wants you to be faithful. Do you know what "faithful" means? It means to keep on doing the job—sticking to it.

Day 9　　　　　　　　　　　　　　Read Ephesians 6:17

Hide and Seek Words ☐

As you read your Bible try to find these hidden words:

"Take the... sword of the Spirit"

Modern Swords

Swords are still used for fighting! And very skillfully—by the swordfish.

A swordfish is from five to fifteen feet long.

As he goes through a school of fish, slashing with his sword, he leaves behind many dead fish for his meal.

There is another sword still in use, too. It is called the "sword of the Spirit" or the Word of God. You need this sword to fight your enemy Satan when he comes to tempt you to do wrong or be unhappy or fearful. Verses in the Bible tell you what to do. They give encouragement. Keep your sword handy. Use it often. Memorize verses from God's Word so you will never be caught without your sword.

Day 10

Read Psalm 40:3

Hide and Seek Words ☐

As you read your Bible try to find these hidden words:

"He hath put a new song in my mouth"

Cheery Songs

Many years ago, King Philip of Spain became ill from unhappiness. Many remedies were tried but nothing seemed to help until someone came to sing in the room next to his. That was the cure he needed: he was soon well.

King Saul of the Bible had times when he felt very unhappy. So he asked David to come and live at his palace and play for him on his harp. This quiet, beautiful music made him feel much better.

A song on your lips can cheer you and those around you, too.

And so when I feel cranky
I bow my head and say,
"Please, dear Jesus, give to me,
A song to sing today!"

— Marjorie Louise Finch

Day 11 Read 1 Peter 5:7

Hide and Seek Words ☐
As you read your Bible try to find these hidden words:

"Casting all your care upon him"

His Loving Care

"Come on, sleepy head; get out of that bed. It's the first day of school. Remember?" Fifteen-year-old Meg playfully grabbed the pillow from under her brother's head and put it on top of his head.

"Don't want to go to this school," his muffled voice came from under the pillow. "Want my old school. I won't know any of the other boys or the teacher. I won't be able to find my room and I'll get lost. And I won't have anyone to play with or eat my lunch with," Kenny wailed.

"Listen, Kenny," Meg said, "I was feeling the same way but Mom showed me a Bible verse and now I feel lots better. It is 'Casting all your care upon him, for he careth for you.' He cares what happens to us today so He will watch over us. Come on, let's trust the Lord Jesus to keep His promise."

Day 12   Read Psalm 23:1

Hide and Seek Words ☐

As you read your Bible try to find these hidden words:

"The Lord is my shepherd"

I'm His Sheep

John was watching a flock of sheep with his uncle. He noticed one old sheep had wandered off and was even that moment stepping over the edge of a bank into the creek below. What was even worse, several other sheep were following right behind.

"I must hurry or soon there will be many sheep in the creek. They will blindly follow the one ahead," John shouted to his uncle. They ran toward the wandering sheep. Soon with the help of their sheep dogs, they had the sheep turned back from danger.

We are like sheep. We are not very wise and choose to follow the wrong leader. Many times we don't know what to do, but the Lord Jesus, our Shepherd, is ready to guide us if we will let Him.

Day 13   Read Proverbs 18:24

Hide and Seek Words ☐
As you read your Bible try to find these hidden words:

"A man that hath friends must show himself friendly"

The Way to Friendship

Many years ago there lived in the mountains of Utah a man by the name of Mr. Ferguson. He lived all by himself in a log cabin except for the animals who recognized him as a friend and kept him company. The birds would come when he called them and eat from his hand. The squirrels played around his feet like kittens.

One day another man came to visit him and said, "You must have some kind of power to tame the animals as you have."

But Mr. Ferguson said, "No, they have learned that I am their friend and will not harm them."

Have you learned the law of having friends, whether they are animals or people? If you wish others to be your friends, you must be friendly to them.

Day 14   Read Galatians 6:10

Hide and Seek Words ☐

As you read your Bible try to find these hidden words:

"... do good unto all men"

Fun to Help

"Lee and I have really had fun today, Mom," Mike said. "After we got our work done here we went over to Grandma Spencer's house. We carried some wood for her fireplace and raked her lawn. Then we carried some groceries home for Mr. Brown; you know, he's crippled. After that, we went to the park and pushed some of the little kids in the swing and helped them go down the slide. We really had fun!"

"I see you've learned the secret," Mother said.

"Secret? Oh, I know, you mean it's fun to help."

"Yes, Mike, and remember in whatever you do or say, you can do it because you love the Lord Jesus." Mother reminded him. "This makes it even more fun. It's like doing it for Him."

Day 15   Read Romans 8:28

Hide and Seek Words ☐
As you read your Bible try to find these hidden words:

"...all things work together for good to them that love God"

A Happy Trade

"You know, Ruth," Carol said as they walked along together. "I didn't like it at first when I had to move. But if I hadn't, then I wouldn't have you for a friend now."

"Yes," Ruth agreed, "and maybe I wouldn't have come to know about the Lord Jesus dying for my sins either, for it was you who took me to the *Good News Club*™ where I learned about receiving the Lord Jesus as my Savior from sin. Now I'm a Christian, too."

"I'm sure glad I moved. I wouldn't want to trade my way for God's way. God knew what was best all along, didn't He?"

> There's a law that I am learning,
> That is helping me each day—
> That our God sends something better,
> For each thing He takes away.

Day 16   Read Matthew 10:31

Hide and Seek Words ☐

As you read your Bible try to find these hidden words:

"...ye are of more value than many sparrows"

He Sees the Sparrows

When God created the earth, He made many beautiful birds. One of the most beautiful is the quetzal. Its crest and upper feathers are mostly metallic green with bright red below. His tail, covered with lacy, fernlike feathers, is often three feet long! The quetzal makes its nest in the trunk of a tree. From the nest there are both front and rear doors, so the daddy bird won't damage his tail when he helps to hatch the eggs. He goes in one door and lets his tail hang outside. When he leaves, he just flies out the other door.

The Lord Jesus made special mention of a bird, but it wasn't a beautiful bird like the quetzal. It was a very plain one—the sparrow. The Lord Jesus notices when one sparrow falls to the ground. Since He notices the common little sparrow, how much more will He notice and watch over His children. You need never fear that He will forget you. You may feel unimportant, but God still cares about you.

Day 17   Read 2 Corinthians 5:17

Hide and Seek Words ☐
As you read your Bible try to find these hidden words:
"... all things are become new"

He Turns the Frown Upside Down

"Sour Sam" is what many people called him. I'm quite sure the neighborhood cats and dogs would have called him that, too, if they could have talked. They almost always got kicked if they tried to get friendly.

One day, though, it almost seemed that there was a new boy on the block.

"Hi, Bob," called Sam, "do you want me to help you mow the lawn?" And, "Here, Billy, do you want some of my candy?" Sam said each sentence with a smile, too. He even treated the animals differently.

Finally, a neighbor asked, "Sam, what makes you so happy now? Did someone give you a thousand dollars?"

"No, sir," Sam smiled happily, "I have received the Lord Jesus as my Savior. He has made the difference. I am glad He has changed my thoughts and actions."

Day 18   Read Luke 5:32

Hide and Seek Words ☐

As you read your Bible try to find these hidden words:

"I came ... to call ... sinners"

God Loves Everyone

"Who was that?" Joe asked his roommate in the hospital.

"That was my pastor," Ron answered.

"So you're a little church boy," Joe sneered.

"Why not? When I think of how much the Lord Jesus loves me, I can't help but love Him."

"He doesn't love me; no one loves me," Joe declared, "but I don't even care."

"God loves you. In fact, He gave His Son the Lord Jesus to die on the cross to take the punishment for your and my sins. All you have to do is ask the Lord Jesus to forgive your sins and ask Him to be your Savior. And He'll forgive you. That's what He did for me."

Joe thought a lot about what Ron told him. He liked the thought of someone loving and caring for him. And before Joe left the hospital, he, too, asked the Lord Jesus to take his sins away. Then he said with a smile, "It's sure neat to know that God loves me, too."

Day 19   Read Luke 11:10

Hide and Seek Words ☐
As you read your Bible try to find these hidden words:

"Everyone that asketh receiveth"

Keep Asking

"Do you suppose Jan will ever receive the Lord Jesus?" Jennifer asked Jeremy. "Seems like we've prayed for her so long and all she does is laugh at us when we say anything about being a Christian or going to church."

"I know," Jeremy replied, "but it is so important. I guess we'd better not give up. You know God promises to answer our prayers but He didn't promise to do it right away."

One month later Jennifer and Jeremy were a pair of happy twins when Jan walked in the house and said, "Hey, kids, guess what; I took Jesus as my Savior at the youth meeting downtown this afternoon. Thanks for praying for me."

The twins grinned happily and in their hearts, whispered, "Thank You, Lord Jesus."

Day 20   Read Joshua 1:9

Hide and Seek Words ☐

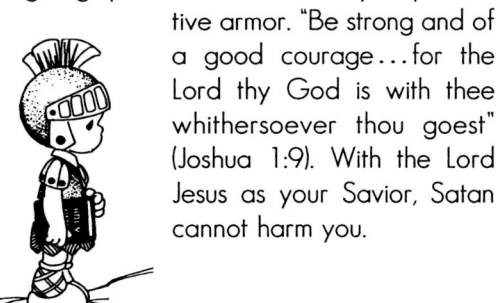

As you read your Bible try to find these hidden words:

"... be not afraid"

First Class Armor

Have you ever seen an armadillo? He's a strange little animal, isn't he? He's covered with a horny armor-like plate like the knights wore long ago. He comes to a point in front, but in back he looks like he's been cut off.

When the armadillo becomes frightened, he digs himself into the sand. His back part becomes an armor plated door of protection.

As a Christian, you need God's armor to protect you from Satan's darts. One of his "darts" is discouragement. He wants you to feel like giving up. Use God's Word as your protective armor. "Be strong and of a good courage...for the Lord thy God is with thee whithersoever thou goest" (Joshua 1:9). With the Lord Jesus as your Savior, Satan cannot harm you.

Day 21   Read Psalm 100:4

Hide and Seek Words ☐
As you read your Bible try to find these hidden words:
"Be thankful unto him"

Every Day—Thanksgiving

"What are you doing, Jeannie?" Mark asked his little sister.

"Making a list of things to be thankful for."

"It's not Thanksgiving," Mark reminded her.

"I know, but my teacher said we shouldn't wait until Thanksgiving to be thankful."

"Guess she's right. Let me see what you have so far—God, Bible, Mother, Father, Brother," he read with a grin. "Eyes, nose, hands, feet, but what is 'tog'?" Mark questioned.

"That's 'tongue'—there are probably more that aren't spelled right. I didn't know I had so many things to be thankful for. And I'm not nearly through."

How many things can you think of to be thankful for? Don't wait until Thanksgiving to say,

Thank You

Day 22 Read James 1:5

Hide and Seek Words ☐
As you read your Bible try to find these hidden words:

**"If any of you lack wisdom
...ask of God"**

How to Get Wise

Barbie sat by the kitchen table, looking miserable. Her math book and paper were in front of her. Suddenly, she burst into tears.

"Mother, I can't understand these problems: I can't—I can't! Both you and Miss Green have tried to explain them to me, but I just *can't* get them!"

"I know it seems impossible," her mother said, "but I know there is one person who could help you if you'd ask Him to. Who is the wisest one in the world?"

"Why, I don't know," Barbie puzzled. "You're wise, but I suppose there are some wiser."

"Yes, indeed," Mother smiled.

"Oh, I know—God."

"Right! And you're His child, aren't you? So why not ask your Heavenly Father to help you understand?"

"All right, Mother, I will." And right there she bowed her head and asked God to help her understand—and of course—He did!

Day 23   Read Psalm 5:3

Hide and Seek Words ☐

As you read your Bible to find these hidden words:

"In the morning will I direct my prayer unto thee"

Morning Strength

"What a morning!" Tommy said as he flopped into a chair at lunchtime. "I did about everything wrong. I even snapped back at my teacher, and my best friend, too. What's wrong with me?"

"I can guess," Mother said. "You got up late this morning and rushed off without eating your breakfast. You had nothing in your tummy to give you strength for the morning."

Tommy nodded his head and said, "I sure was hungry and tired."

"It is important," Mother said, "to take time for breakfast, but even more important to take time to talk to God and let Him talk with you. You need spiritual strength for your day, too."

"You're right, Mom. I want the afternoon to be different." Tommy bowed his head and told God he was sorry for losing his temper and for not taking time for things that were really important. "Help me to get up when mother calls and get my day started off right tomorrow!"

Day 24   Read Hebrews 13:5

Hide and Seek Words ☐
As you read your Bible try to find these hidden words:
"Be content with such things as ye have"

Be Content

Paul and Silas were thrown into prison after being beaten. Was it because they were bad men? No. They had done what the Lord Jesus wanted them to do, and wicked men had become angry. But Paul and Silas did something very surprising; they prayed and sang praises to God. They were even happy in jail because they knew God loved them and wouldn't let anything happen to them without a good reason. Boys and girls today have learned this, too.

Mickey was thrilled with her Christmas bike, even though it was a used one, until her best friend came spinning along on her brand-new, shiny one. Then Mickey began feeling bad because her bike wasn't new, too. When she realized what ugly thoughts were coming into her mind, she asked the Lord Jesus to forgive her and help her to be thankful. After all, she knew her mother and dad had bought her the best they could afford. The Lord Jesus did help her too, for soon she was happy and thankful again.

Day 25   Read Matthew 19:26

Hide and Seek Words ☐

As you read your Bible try to find these hidden words:

"With God all things are possible"

Do the Impossible

"I just can't stand her!" Megan angrily looked back at Melody riding away on a new bike. "She thinks she's so smart; just because her parents can afford to give her nicer things. *'Your father,'* she says, *'must have bought your bike at a fourth-hand store; not a second-hand one.'* Oh, I just hate her!"

"Oh, Megan, you mustn't hate anyone," her friend Gail said.

"Well, I just can't help it."

"Can't help what?" asked an old gentleman hobbling by with his cane.

"Oh, something," Megan smiled in spite of herself. "It's just that some things are impossible."

"Not with God's help," the old man said as he shuffled on.

Not with God's help. The words stayed with Megan. And it was true too; as she prayed, God helped her to do the impossible—to love Melody who had been unkind to her.

Day 26   Read Matthew 6:8

Hide and Seek Words ☐
As you read your Bible try to find these hidden words:

**"Your Father knoweth
what things ye need"**

No! No! No!

"No, no, Justin, you can't have that."

Justin was angry when the knife was placed out of reach. But all Jeannie said was, "Stop crying, Justin; you could hurt yourself."

Sometimes we ask God for something and wonder why He will not give it to us.

The apostle Paul had something which bothered him. He asked God to take it from him but God said, "no." Paul knew God loved him and had a good reason for not giving him his wishes.

REMEMBER
There's always a reason,
It's nice to know,
When though you pray hard,
God must answer, "no."
You pray for the things
You think you'd like best;
God sends what's good for you,
And cancels the rest.
So don't get discouraged,
Trust God when you pray;
He'll answer your pleadings
In the very best way!

Day 27 Read Galatians 6:2

Hide and Seek Words ☐

As you read your Bible try to find these hidden words:

"Bear ye one another's burdens"

Burden Bearers

"How do you like our country, Min-Su?" Rick asked the Korean boy who had only been in the United States for about six months.

"I would like it better if I didn't have such a bad time with the schoolwork," he said. "I thought I knew a lot about your language before I left Korea but now I'm not so sure. I cannot understand many of the words in your books."

"Hm-m-m, we'll have to do something about that. How would it be if some of the fellows would help you in the evenings with your homework, by explaining the words you don't understand?"

"Oh, would you?" Min-Su smiled in relief. "You don't know how much better that makes me feel!"

Helping others when they are having a hard time is one way to bear another's burdens.

Day 28   Read Matthew 5:44

Hide and Seek Words □

As you read your Bible try to find these hidden words:

**"Love your enemies,
...and pray for them"**

The Christian's Weapons

The Bombardier beetle declares gas warfare when he sees an enemy. He has a sac at the end of his body which, when squeezed, sounds like a pop-gun. His "bullet" is a cloud of vapor which stings and blinds.

The porcupine fish uses needles to protect himself. If he sees an enemy approaching, he inflates himself like a balloon, making sharp spines stand out all over him. A Christian's weapons are not like these.

Bobby had a rough time when Pete was around, for Pete loved to pick on the boys who were smaller—especially Bobby. But Bobby decided to treat him as the Lord Jesus would: he prayed for him. And when Pete became sick it was Bobby who took him his school books and loaned him his games, books, and puzzles. Bobby showed real love for Pete. Now Pete isn't Bobby's enemy; he is his protector and friend.

Day 29

Read Psalm 103:3

Hide and Seek Words ☐

As you read your Bible try to find these hidden words:

"Who forgiveth all thine iniquities [sins]"

Every Bit Forgiven

"What's the matter, Jean?" Jon asked, when he found his sister crying.

"I–I–feel so awful!" she sobbed. "This terrible temper of mine! I didn't mean for Joey to get so badly hurt when I pushed him. Now he's in the hospital with a broken arm. I don't think anyone will forgive me this time—even the Lord Jesus." And Jean cried harder than ever.

"Oh, come on Jean, you know He will. The Bible says, 'If we confess our sins, he is faithful and just to forgive us our sins, and to cleanse us from *ALL* unrighteousness' (1 John 1:9). And if the Bible says 'all' that is just exactly what it means. Have you told the Lord Jesus you're sorry?"

"Yes," Jean whispered.

"Then He's forgiven you; He promised. Why don't you thank Him and dry your tears," Jon said as he ruffled her hair. "And, I'll go with you to see Joey at the hospital, too."

Day 30   Read Psalm 95:6

Hide and Seek Words ☐
As you read your Bible try to find these hidden words:

"... let us worship and bow down"

A Proper Time for Everything

"How's fishing?" Pastor Johnson asked as he joined Randy at the edge of Silver Lake.

"Not bad," Randy answered. "A lot better than it was Sunday morning, anyway." Randy's face suddenly got red as he realized he had given himself away!

"I guess I really shouldn't have gone with the other boys Sunday morning, but they said it was so much fun other Sundays."

"Did you enjoy it?" his pastor asked.

"Nah; I was miserable and haven't felt right ever since."

"That's because you are a Christian and your place is in church on Sunday. You need that time set aside to worship and learn about the Lord Jesus. And it's good to be with others who love Him. We can encourage one another."

"I know you're right, Pastor Johnson. I'm glad you stopped by. And I'll be back next week."

Maranatha

Day 1   1 Corinthians 16:22

Hide and Seek Words ☐
As you read your Bible try to find these hidden words:
"Maranatha [our Lord is coming]"

What's the Password?

Have you ever been a member of a secret club? If so, you probably had a password which only members of your club knew. Nobody else knew what it meant!

Once believers in the Lord Jesus Christ had a password! The Lord Jesus had died for sins, been buried, and had risen from the grave. Before He went back to Heaven, He promised His followers He would come back again. The password of the early believers in the Lord Jesus was Maranatha. Maranatha means "our Lord is coming!"

Often believers were treated badly by their enemies. Some were beaten. Some were even killed. Believers would cheer each other up by saying "Maranatha" when they met. Sometimes they had to meet secretly. They knew when they heard the password *Maranatha* that those coming to the meeting were believers too!

Day 2   Read Matthew 13:11

Hide and Seek Words ☐
As you read your Bible try to find these hidden words:

"... know the mysteries"

Solving a Mystery

When people who did not believe in the Lord Jesus heard believers say "Maranatha," they didn't know what they meant. *Maranatha* was a mystery to them. Many things in the Bible may seem like mysteries. Let's see if we can solve some. Finding out about the Lord's coming will be our "mystery story"! Each day we'll talk about another clue. The clue will be something that has happened or will happen.

All our clues are in the Bible (In God's Word, we find the answers to all our problems.) The Bible tells us how we can have our sins forgiven by receiving the Lord Jesus Christ. It tells us how to live to please Him.

By studying God's Word, we can understand more about Him and His plans. We can know the mysteries.

Day 3   Read John 3:16

Hide and Seek Words ☐

As you read your Bible try to find these hidden words:

"... whosoever believeth ... have everlasting life"

A Family Reunion

When you were in a secret club, did everyone you knew belong? No, it was only those who were invited. Did all those who were asked to join, do it? Did they have to? I don't suppose they did. A club is a special group who belong because they want to.

God's special group is *not* secret! He has invited everyone. If you have received the Lord Jesus as your Savior from sin, you belong to God's special group—His family. Perhaps your secret club did not last very long, but if you belong to God's family, it's forever. He gives everlasting life. Some day there will be a great big family reunion in Heaven. (That's part of our mystery story.)

Day 4   Read Matthew 27:63

Hide and Seek Words ☐

As you read your Bible try to find these hidden words:

"I will rise again"

He Lives

Today our mystery clue is a word: resurrection (res er reck shun). Resurrection means "risen from the dead." Many had seen Jesus raise other people from the dead. And they should have believed that He could raise Himself from the dead, too, for the Lord Jesus is God. The Bible tells us Jesus told His disciples He would be killed but that He would rise again on the third day (Matthew 16:21).

After Jesus was buried, some of His enemies said, "We remember that that deceiver said... After three days I will rise again." Guards were placed at the tomb to be sure the disciples could not steal Jesus' body and pretend He was alive. But the guards could not keep the Lord Jesus from rising from the dead. Remember, *resurrection;* we'll see that word again.

Day 5   Read Acts 1:11

Hide and Seek Words ☐
As you read your Bible try to find these hidden words:
"This same Jesus... will come again"

He's Coming

The Lord Jesus is the Son of God. He had always lived in Heaven with God the Father until one day He came to earth where He was born as a baby. He then had a body like ours.

After the Lord Jesus grew to be a man, He told people He would die and rise again. When He was nailed to a cross where He died, many people did not understand how He could be the Savior. But when He rose from the grave, those who had believed on Him remembered He had promised that He would rise again.

One day the Lord Jesus was out on a hill with some of the believers. Suddenly He rose up into the air and disappeared! He went back to Heaven. He sent messengers to tell His disciples that someday He would come back. He didn't say when this would be. Ever since that time, those who have received the Lord Jesus have been looking for Him.

Have you received Him as your Savior? Are you looking for Him to come?

Day 6   Read John 14:2

Hide and Seek Words ☐
As you read your Bible try to find these hidden words:

"In my Father's house are many mansions"

We're Moving

"We're moving, Mark," Dad said. "We're going to live with Grandfather in his big, beautiful house in California." Dad had lived there when he was a boy. But Mark had never seen the place. He'd only heard stories about it! Big house with lots of rooms! A stream! Apple trees! Room for a horse! Mark could hardly wait to move.

While the Lord Jesus was on earth, He told His disciples He was going back to Heaven to His Father's house. There are many mansions or rooms in the Heavenly Father's house. There is room for every one who receives the Lord Jesus as Savior from sin. Have you received Him? Are you looking forward to moving to the Father's house in Heaven?

Day 7   Read John 14:2

Hide and Seek Words ☐
As you read your Bible try to find these hidden words:
"I go to prepare a place for you"

Getting Ready

Mark, his mother, and father talked much about the move to Grandfather's. Dad went on ahead to see about his new job. He would also find out if the house needed any changes or repairs. He said he would let them know if they should pack any of their own furniture. "As soon as everything is ready," he said, "I'll be back to get you." Mark knew he was going to enjoy living at Grandfather's.

When the Lord Jesus told His disciples He was going back to His Father's house, He said, "I go to prepare a place for you." We don't know what that means, for we know Heaven is already perfect. But whatever it is, it will be special for each one of us.

What Heaven is like seems a mystery now. But won't it be exciting to see what it is like?

Day 8   Read John 14:3

Hide and Seek Words ☐
As you read your Bible try to find these hidden words:
"... where I am, there you may be also"

With Him

Mark's father had been gone for several days. Mark missed his dad. Mother missed him, too. But they knew he was getting everything ready for them. Then he would come for them. And they would travel together to Grandfather's big house. Mark was glad Father was coming for them because Grandfather's house was so far away. Both Mother and Mark would often say, "I'll be glad when Dad comes and we can go to be with him."

When the Lord Jesus told His disciples He was going to prepare a place for them, He also said, "I will come again and take you with me that where I am there you may be also."

How wonderful it will be to be with the Lord Jesus forever. *Maranatha!*

Day 9   Read John 9:4

Hide and Seek Words ☐

As you read your Bible try to find these hidden words:

"I must work . . . while it is day"

Much to Be Done

Finally a letter came. "No need for any of our furniture," Dad wrote. Mother and Mark kept on sorting the things they would keep and the things they would sell or give away. There was much to do before Mark's Dad came for them.

Before the Lord Jesus went back to Heaven, He told His disciples what He wanted them to do. "Go into all the world and preach...," He said. They were to tell others about Him. They were to watch—be expecting Him to come any time; they were to love one another; they were to do good. As you study God's Word, He will show you things He wants you to do in living your life pleasing to Him. Ask Him to show you something you can do for Him today.

Day 10   Read 2 Peter 3:9

Hide and Seek Words ☐
As you read your Bible try to find these hidden words:

**"The Lord is not slack
concerning his promise"**

But When?

After his father had been gone for some time, Mark began to ask, "When is Dad coming? When will everything be ready so we can move to Grandfather's?" Mother would reply, "It won't be very long. As soon as he is ready, he will come."

Some of Mark's friends said, "Maybe your father isn't coming back." But Mark knew this was not true. He knew his father would come, even if it took a long time.

People who do not believe in the Lord Jesus sometimes make fun of those who have received Him as Savior from sin and say, "When is Jesus coming back? You've been saying He would come for a long time." The Bible says, "God is not slack...not slow concerning his promise." It seems slow to us, but with God a thousand years isn't any longer than a day with us.

At the right time, the Lord Jesus will come, just as He said He would.

Day 11   Read 1 John 2:28

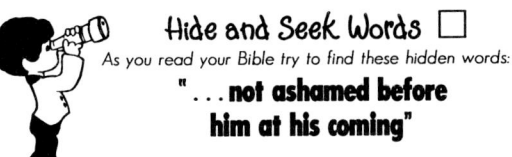

Hide and Seek Words ☐

As you read your Bible try to find these hidden words:

". . . not ashamed before him at his coming"

If You Obey

"Father will be coming sometime today," Mother said to Mark. "So stay home and keep clean." Mark waited all morning. When he went outside after lunch, he looked up and down the street. There was no sign of his father's car. Mark heard some of his friends playing ball in the vacant lot. He just planned to watch, but soon he had joined in the game. Running to catch the ball, Mark stumbled and fell in a mud puddle. Next thing he knew, someone yelled, "Hey, Mark, there's your dad's car."

Mark ran as fast as he could, sneaking into the back door. If only he could get to his room and change his clothes before Dad saw him. But then he remembered—his clothes were all packed. Father was standing in the doorway. Mark was so ashamed. Dad knew he had not obeyed.

If you obey God, you'll not be ashamed when the Lord Jesus comes.

Day 12   Read 1 Thessalonians 4:16

Hide and Seek Words ☐

As you read your Bible try to find these hidden words:

"...the Lord himself shall descend from heaven"

How?

How will the Lord Jesus come? Our clue is in Acts 1:11. Remember, the messengers said He will come the same way He went. How did He go? Up in the air. How will He come? The Bible says, "the Lord himself will descend [come down] from heaven." We read stories about people floating through the air and suddenly appearing in a room. That is all make-believe. No earth person could do that. When the Lord Jesus lived on earth, He had an earth body too. Now He has a resurrection body—a real space body.

The disciples saw the Lord go up to Heaven. They saw the messengers who said He would return.

We know these things are true because God's Word tells us so. Someday soon we may see for ourselves—see the Lord Himself descend from Heaven.

Day 13   Read 1 Thessalonians 4:16

Hide and Seek Words ☐
As you read your Bible try to find these hidden words:
"... with a shout"

The Signal

Boys and girls used to play a game called *Run, Sheep, Run.* It was like *Hide-and-Seek* with two teams. The captain of the hiding team would come back to base and go with the searching team. The captain of the hiding team would call secret signals so his team would know where the searchers were. When he thought his team could get to base first, he would shout, "Run, sheep, run." That was the signal to go—and go fast. No trying now to find a better hiding place, or stop to tie your shoe.

The Bible says, "the Lord himself shall descend from heaven with a shout, with the voice of the archangel, and with the trump of God."

When we hear the Lord's shout, it will be like Him saying, "Here I come, ready or not." Are you ready?

Day 14 | 1 Thessalonians 4:16

Hide and Seek Words ☐
As you read your Bible try to find these hidden words:

"...the dead in Christ shall rise first"

We Shall Live Again

What's going to happen when the Lord gives the signal? The Bible tells us that the believers who have already died will be raised from the dead.

Remember our mystery word on the 4th day? It was *resurrection*. Just as the Lord Jesus rose again from the dead, those who believe on Him will also be raised from their graves.

If you should die before the Lord Jesus comes again, your body will be placed in a grave. But when He gives the signal, your body will be raised from the grave; it will be changed into a body like that of the Lord Jesus; and you will be caught up to meet Him in the air. God's Word says it will all happen in the "twinkling of an eye." You will be with Him.

Day 15   Read 1 Thessalonians 4:17

Hide and Seek Words ☐

As you read your Bible try to find these hidden words:

"... we shall be caught up"

Space Trip

...three...two...one...blast off! A spaceship is launched—streaking toward the moon. Astronauts travel further than anyone has ever gone before—further than dreamed possible before the first spacecraft was built.

How would you like to be an astronaut and fly way out in space? It must be very exciting! But when the Lord Jesus returns, something much more exciting will happen! Yesterday we talked about those who believe in Jesus who have already died. They will be raised from their graves. But those of us who have received the Lord Jesus and are still alive will be caught up with them to meet the Lord Jesus in the air.

How fast? In the twinkling of an eye. Faster than astronauts will ever go in a spaceship.

Day 16   Read 1 Corinthians 15:51

Hide and Seek Words ☐

As you read your Bible try to find these hidden words:

"... we shall all be changed"

Space Bodies

Ready for another mystery? When the Lord Jesus comes back, how do you suppose we will be able to fly through outer space? You could flap your arms and jump up and down all day, but you couldn't fly.

Have you ever seen a fuzzy caterpillar fly? At a certain time in a caterpillar's life, he spins a blanket, called a cocoon, around himself. He goes to sleep; then when he wakes up he squeezes out of his cocoon. He can fly for he has turned into a butterfly!

Someday, if the Lord Jesus does not come before that, you will die. I will die. Our bodies will be placed in graves. When the Lord Jesus gives the signal, all the believers who have died will be raised, alive again. They will have new bodies. Space bodies. Those who are still living will also be given new bodies like the body of the Lord Jesus so that we may travel with Him.

Day 17   Read Mark 11:9

Hide and Seek Words

As you read your Bible try to find these hidden words:

"Blessed is he that cometh"

Puzzle

Find the missing words in verses, or stories, you read for other days in this booklet Place answers in the squares above.

1. Study God's Word to understand the ____ (Day 2).
2. Jesus will come ____ (Day 5).
3. The mystery word ____ (Day 4).
4. Jesus said, "You may be where I ___ (Day 8).
5. Our Lord will come from ___ (Day 12).
6. We don't want to be ___ (Day 11).
7. Our Lord will signal with a ___ (Day 13).
8. There are many mansions in the Father's ___ (Day 6).
9. We shall ____ be changed (Day 26).
10. the Password ___ (Day 1).

(Answers on last page)

Day 18   Read 1 Corinthians 15:52

Hide and Seek Words □

As you read your Bible try to find these hidden words:

"... the dead shall be raised incorruptible"

Never Die Again

Have you ever had to empty a vase of dead flowers? They smelled bad, didn't they? Especially if the water had not been changed on them. Once they were beautiful—smelled sweet. But when they died, they smelled bad. Flowers are corruptible. Today's mystery word—incorruptible—means just the opposite. Things which are incorruptible can't die. Can't get rotten. Can't smell bad. Can't get spoiled. That's what our new bodies will be like. Imagine it. They will never get sick. Never have pain. Never have an ache anywhere—not even in a little toe! Our new bodies will be just like Jesus' resurrection body. Our new bodies will be *incorruptible*.

Day 19 Read 1 Thessalonians 4:17

Hide and Seek Words

As you read your Bible try to find these hidden words:

"...so shall we ever be with the Lord"

With Him

The best thing about Heaven is that we will be with the Lord Jesus forever. The Lord Jesus told His disciples, "In my Father's house are many mansions: if it were not so, I would have told you. I go to prepare a place for you. And if I go and prepare a place for you, I will come again, and receive you unto myself; that where I am, there you may be also" (John 14:2, 3).

Heaven is a wonderful place. There will be no riots, no sickness, no sorrow, because there will be no sin in Heaven. Heaven will be like a king's palace, for God's throne is there! Heaven may seem mysterious now, but when we get there, all the mystery will be gone. God's Word does not tell us every thing about Heaven but of one thing we can be certain—we shall be with the Lord Jesus forever.

Day 20 Read Romans 14:12

Hide and Seek Words ☐
As you read your Bible try to find these hidden words:

"...every one...shall give account of himself to God"

Report Time

One day Father gave Michael and Ben some money. "At the end of the week I want you to give an account of how you have spent the money," he said.

"What's an account?" Ben asked.

"It's a report—a checkup—on what you've done. If it shows you've spent your money wisely, I'll give you each a reward."

What do you think they did with their money? We'll be meeting them again tomorrow.

But did you know that you will have to give an account to the Lord Jesus as to how you use your time and your money? What you do shows just how much you really love Him. You must give your own report.

Day 21   Read 1 Corinthians 3:15

Hide and Seek Words ☐
As you read your Bible try to find these hidden words:

"If any man's work be burned, he shall suffer loss"

All Gone

When Father asked Michael and Ben to give an account of how they had spent the money, Michael said, "I bought a lot of balloons and a lot of candy. First time I ever had so much all for myself."

"Where are your things?" Father asked.

"Oh," Michael said sadly, "the balloons all popped and I ate all the candy. They're all gone."

The things we do only for ourselves, in our own way, are like wood, hay, and stubble. Fire can easily burn those things. The things we do for God, in His way, are like gold, silver and precious stones. Fire cannot burn them.

How will the things you do today stand God's test?

Day 22   Read 1 Corinthians 3:14

Hide and Seek Words ☐
As you read your Bible try to find these hidden words:
"If any man's work abide . . . he shall receive a reward"

Giving That Lasts

When Ben gave an account of the money his father had given him, he said, "I bought some candy and shared it with Matthew. He never has much of anything like that. And then I got a model airplane set. And I saved some money to put in the missionary bank."

"Your candy is gone, but you made someone else happy by sharing. You will learn things by making up your model plane, as well as have fun with it. And the money you give for missions will keep on working. Someone else will hear about the Lord Jesus and may receive Him as Savior. You have used your money wisely. So I shall give you an allowance starting next week."

What you do for others is really doing it for the Lord Jesus. The Bible says, "If any man's work abide [lasts] . . . he shall receive a reward."

Day 23   Read 2 Corinthians 5:10

Hide and Seek Words ☐
As you read your Bible try to find these hidden words:

"... we must all appear before the judgment seat of Christ"

The Judge

A judge is a man who sits in court and listens to what is said for and against someone who broke the law. If the person is guilty, the judge decides what his punishment should be. But a judge is also someone who decides the winner in a contest. If you had a contest at school to see who could make the best drawing, the judge would examine all the drawings. He would decide which was best. The best one would earn a reward.

Someday the Lord Jesus is going to judge all things you have done. He will decide if you have earned any rewards. The place where the Lord Jesus will do this is called the judgment seat of Christ. Every believer will have to appear before the judgment seat of Christ to give an account.

Day 24 Read 1 Corinthians 9:25

Hide and Seek Words ☐

As you read your Bible try to find these hidden words:

"...an incorruptible crown"

A Crown?

One of our mystery words was *incorruptible* (Day 18). *Crown* is our mystery word today. You may think of the crown that a king wears. But there is another meaning. It can mean the highest honor. Long ago an athlete who won a race was given a wreath of leaves. It was placed on his head to show he was being honored. The Bible says that living for the Lord Jesus is like running a race. If we do what pleases the Lord Jesus, we will receive an honor or a crown. But we must live according to God's rules.

The crown of leaves the athlete received was corruptible—it would spoil, fade away and die. But we will win an incorruptible crown, a reward that will not fade away.

Day 25　　　　　　　Read 1 Thessalonians 2:19

Hide and Seek Words ☐
As your read your Bible try to find these hidden words:

"... our ... crown of rejoicing"

Will You Rejoice?

Mystery word—*rejoicing*. What does the middle part sound like? *Joy*. Rejoicing means "showing our joy—showing how glad we are." God's Word says there is joy in Heaven when even one person receives the Lord Jesus Christ (Luke 15:7, 10).

The missionary Paul called some people who had received the Lord Jesus as Savior his crown of rejoicing. When you tell someone of the Lord Jesus and he receives Him as Savior from sin, both of you are made glad.

If a person does not receive the Lord Jesus as Savior, he will not be able to go to Heaven. Maranatha would not be a happy saying for him. Remember what this word means?

Day 26　　　　　　　　　　Read 2 Timothy 4:8

Hide and Seek Words ☐

As you read your Bible try to find these hidden words:

"... there is laid up for me a crown of righteousness"

Are You Glad?

One morning Mother said, "Today Uncle Bill will take you to the farm to stay while your father and I are away. He won't have time to wait, so be sure to be ready."

"Oh, I'm glad," Rebecca called, as she hurried to finish her chores.

"I don't want to go," Shelley pouted as she got ready.

Gary said, "Great." But Gary played most of the morning and didn't get all of his things ready. He had to leave some.

Which one of the children was glad to see Uncle Bill?

God promises a crown of righteousness to all who love His appearing—His coming. Righteousness is being right the way God wants us to be right.

If you are looking forward to the Lord Jesus' coming, you will want to be doing those things you know please Him.

Day 27   Read 1 Peter 5:4

Hide and Seek Words ☐

As you read your Bible try to find these hidden words:

"...ye shall receive a crown of glory"

A Leader

Mystery word—*glory*. It means brightness and it may mean honor. This is a special crown for special work. It could be for missionaries, pastors, or teachers. To be a leader when you grow up, you must prepare while you are young. You can learn God's Word so you can help someone else understand it. You can encourage other boys and girls to go to Sunday school or Good News Club.™ You can show others by the way you live what it means to obey God!

If you are helpful in leading the way to God, being an example, helping others to learn and obey God's Word, you, too, may have a crown of glory.

Day 28   Read James 1:12

Hide and Seek Words ☐

As you read your Bible try to find these hidden words:

"...he shall receive the crown of life"

Trust God

Endure is a good mystery word. Suppose someone tries to get you to do wrong. First, you say *no*. But he says, "Aw, come on, it's fun." You still say *no*. Maybe he makes fun of you, or even hurts you. Finally, you do it. You did not endure. Maybe you are trying to do something right, or good, but it seems too hard, and you give up. You did not endure. Endure means not to give up, not to give in. God promises the crown of life to whoever endures temptation.

Your enemy Satan will tempt you not to trust God—not to obey Him. He will tempt you to give up when it's hard to do right.

God is living in you. He is ready to give you strength to keep on—to endure—when you are tempted to give up. Trust God.

Day 29   Read Revelation 4:10

Hide and Seek Words ☐
As you read your Bible try to find these hidden words:

"...cast their crowns before the throne"

Giving Back

Ever want to give a special present to your father on his birthday? You had no money, but you started doing special jobs and saving as much money as you could. You did your work well—you were paid. You didn't have to spend the money on Father, but you bought a present. You did it because you loved him.

The Bible tells us that in Heaven people will place their crowns before the throne of God. We have nothing really good enough to give Him to show our love. But we can give back to Him those crowns which we earn by obeying Him.

"Thou art worthy, O Lord, to receive glory and honor" (Revelation 4:11).

Day 30   Read Revelation 22:20

Hide and Seek Words ☐
As you read your Bible try to find these hidden words:

"Surely I come..."

Is It the Crowning Day?

Jesus may come today, Glad day! Glad day!

And I would see my friend

Dangers and troubles would end

If Jesus should come today.

Glad day! Glad day! Is it the crowning day?

I'll live for today, nor anxious be

Jesus my Lord I soon shall see

Glad day! Glad day! Is it the crowning day?

Faithful I'll be today, Glad day! Glad day!

And I will freely tell

Why I should love Him so well,

For He is my all today.

Answers to puzzle from Day 17.

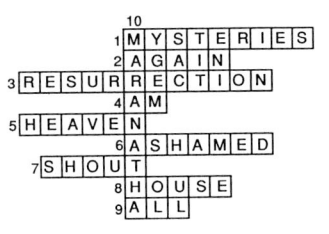

			10					
1	M	Y	S	T	E	R	I	E	S
	2	A	G	A	I	N		
3	R	E	S	U	R	R	E	C	T	I	O	N
		4	A	M				
5	H	E	A	V	E	N		
		6	A	S	H	A	M	E	D
7	S	H	O	U	T			
	8	H	O	U	S	E		
	9	A	L	L				

Be Attitudes

Day 1   2 Corinthians 5:17

Hide and Seek Words ☐

As you read your Bible try to find these hidden words:

"...in Christ...all things are become new"

Brand New!

When someone receives the Lord Jesus Christ as Savior from sin, he becomes a new person inside. He does not think the same way he did before. A new life begins!

"Don't you see the difference?" David asked his Sunday school teacher.

"Why, yes," she said. "You haven't been fighting or swearing lately. And you have been helping Peter with his workbook. What happened?"

"I did what you said. I asked the Lord Jesus to be my Savior and take away my sins. And He did! My schoolteacher noticed the difference, too."

Do you have the new life that Jesus gives? Do your family and friends notice that you are a different person by the things you say and do?

Day 2   Read Proverbs 23:7a

Hide and Seek Words ☐

As you read your Bible try to find these hidden words:

"... as he thinketh in his heart, so is he"

Inside Out!

An *attitude* is the way you think about something. God says that the way you think will soon show on the outside!

Why do you fight with someone? Because first of all you may have *thought* something like this: "I don't like what he did" or "I'm not going to let her be first all the time." If someone sees a grouchy look on your face, it's because you have been grumbling on the inside. But if you are smiling, it is because you have happy thoughts. You act the way you think!

One day the Lord Jesus sat down along a mountainside and talked with His disciples. He told them eight ways that they should think and why they would be happy if they did. We call the instructions He gave the BE-attitudes. Jesus knows that if you have good thoughts or attitudes, you will say and *do* those things which please Him.

> Welcome good attitudes. Let them stay.
> Ask God to take the bad ones away.

Day 3   Read Matthew 5:1-3

Hide and Seek Words □

As you read your Bible try to find these hidden words:

"Blessed"

Happiness Is...

Do you remember what the BE-attitudes are? (Eight ways that the Lord Jesus wants us to think.) Each Beatitude begins with the word *blessed*. *Blessed* means *happy*. God wants every Christian to be blessed.

"Happiness is a chocolate ice cream cone," said a boy with sparkling brown eyes. But what happens to that happy feeling when the ice cream is gone? The happiness that God gives lasts longer than ice cream, or candy, or even a special vacation trip!

Real happiness is *when you please God*. When you know God is pleased with you, you have a happiness deep in your heart that no one can take away. Each day in your Quiet Time this month, you will read about the BE-attitudes that please God.

Happiness is to know the Savior,
Living a life within His favor,
Having a change in my behavior—
Happiness is the Lord.

© Copyright 1968 by Singspiration/ASCAP. All rights reserved. Used by permission of the Benson Music Group, Inc.

Day 4   Read Matthew 5:1-3

Hide and Seek Words ☐
As you read your Bible try to find these hidden words:

"Blessed are the poor in spirit"

Always Needed!

The Lord Jesus showed us what it means to be "poor in spirit." While He was here on earth, He took many hours to talk with God the Father.

Could it be that you let a long time go by without praying? Did you skip the Bible verses that you were to read today? That is like saying to God, "I can get along without Your help sometimes." But Jesus told His followers, "Without Me you can do NOTHING!"

Doug was not a happy Christian. One day the teacher asked, "Doug, do you have your Quiet Time every day?"

"Well," he answered, "there's scouts after school; then I have to help Mother; then there's homework; and I like to watch TV. There just isn't enough time!"

Happy are the *poor in spirit*—those who take time to ask for God's help. If Doug had taken time to spend with God, he could have been a happier Christian.

Day 5   Read Matthew 5:1-3

Hide and Seek Words ☐
As you read your Bible try to find these hidden words:

"Theirs is the kingdom of heaven"

An Exciting Day!

The "poor in spirit" know they cannot please God themselves. They trust the Lord Jesus to help them say "No" to Satan and "Yes" to God each day. They give God credit for the good things that happen in their lives.

Those who are "poor in spirit" may be great and important in the world. Or they may be just like you and me. But they are happy. Those who trust in God are happy; *someday* they will help to rule the earth!

When the Lord Jesus comes to earth again, there will be a heavenly kingdom here for 1,000 years. When the Lord Jesus becomes king, there will at last be PEACE over all the world. And listen to this—all those who have believed on the Lord Jesus will help Him to rule His kingdom!" ... theirs is the kingdom of heaven." What an exciting day that will be!

> Mine eyes have seen the glory
> Of the coming of the Lord...
> His truth is marching on.
>   —Howe

Day 6   Read Matthew 5:4

Hide and Seek Words ☐

As you read your Bible try to find these hidden words:

"Blessed are they that mourn"

"Weeping Willow"

They called her "Weeping Willow." It was not a nice name. But she cried in the morning. She didn't like her breakfast. She couldn't find her clothes and she cried. She cried when she left for school and she cried when she came home. When Mother said, "You can't do that," she cried. This was not the kind of sadness the Lord Jesus was talking about when He said, "Blessed are they that mourn!"

One day "Weeping Willow" (whose real name was Kimberly) heard about the Lord Jesus. "Jesus died for *your* sins," *the* teacher said. Again Kimberly cried. But this was different. She was crying because she had sinned. It was sin to disobey her mother. It was sin to stamp her foot and demand her own way. Kimberly was truly mourning—she was sorry for her sins. And she asked the Lord Jesus to forgive her.

Happy are those who mourn (are sorry) because of sin—and stop it!

Be attitude 2

Day 7 — Read Psalm 126:5, 6

Hide and Seek Words ☐

As you read your Bible try to find these hidden words:

"He that ... weepeth ... shall ... come again with rejoicing"

Crying for Others

One cloudy day Jack and his sister Carol were playing in the living room. Carol soon tired of her doll, and started to climb on the furniture. She knew Mother had said not to, but she climbed from a chair to the top of the TV set. Somehow she lost her balance and grabbed the floor lamp as she fell. Carol screamed! Mother came running into the room. Carol was screaming but unhurt. Tears were rolling down Jack's cheeks. He felt bad that his sister had disobeyed and that the lamp had been broken. He took his mother's hand. Looking up into her face he asked, "Don't you think we'd better pray?" Mother agreed. She picked Carol up and the three of them knelt by the sofa.

"Please, Lord Jesus," Jack prayed, "help Carol to want to be good. Help us to obey, and help Mommy not to be angry. Amen."

Do the sins of others bring tears to your eyes? God loves your friends, too. He wants them to trust Him as their Savior too.

Day 8   Read John 20:11-13

Hide and Seek Words ☐

As you read your Bible try to find these hidden words:

"They shall be comforted"

Jesus, the Comforter

The Lord Jesus was dead. Mary saw His body wrapped in graveclothes. She watched while they laid Him in the grave. Now she sat by that same grave. But His body was no longer there. Where was He? Suddenly Jesus came. He spoke. He was alive! Mary was comforted—no longer sad.

"Mommy, why are crying?" Larry asked.

"Oh, just because of Cheryl," Mother answered.

"You don't have to cry about her, you know," he comforted gently. "She's in Heaven with the Lord Jesus."

"Yes, I know, Larry. I'm not feeling sorry for Cheryl. But I miss her."

Larry added, "We have sadness down here right now, don't we? Cheryl has a lot more happiness than we have."

Larry was right. They did have sadness. But Larry's mother decided, "Now Heaven seems closer and dearer." The Lord Jesus comforted Mother's heart.

Day 9   Read Matthew 5:4, 5

Hide and Seek Words

As you read your Bible try to find these hidden words:

"Blessed are the meek"

No Complaints!

Diane didn't walk very much. She just hopped and skipped and jumped—a happy girl, who was hardly still a minute. But one day the doctor discovered some trouble in Diane's hip. Unless something was done quickly she would become crippled.

The hopping, skipping, jumping girl was taken to a hospital, strapped to a board, and heavy weights hung from both legs. Then she was put into a cast. For nearly a year she would not be able to walk—or hop, or skip or jump!

Still Diane was happy. She loved the Lord Jesus. Her family loved Him, too. There was no grumbling, complaining or fighting against God. Happy are the meek—those who don't get angry when trouble comes!

Long ago a blind girl wrote:

How many blessings I enjoy,
That other people don't.
To weep and sigh because I'm blind.
I cannot and I won't.
  —F. Crosby

BE attitude 3

Day 10   Read Matthew 11:28-30

Hide and Seek Words ☐
As you read your Bible try to find these hidden words:
"I am meek and lowly in heart"

Waiting for God

A meek person is gentle, humble, and patient.

"We will make Him king! We will make Him king!"

The crowd was excited and noisy. They had just been part of a wonderful miracle. More than 5,000 people had been fed with a boy's lunch. And the Lord Jesus did it! "We will make Jesus king," they said. But when they looked for Him He was not there.

The meek Lord Jesus had hurried away from the crowd. He went into the mountain to be alone—to talk with God the Father. It was not time for Jesus to be king. He would be patient and wait for that for a long time.

First the Lord Jesus had to die for our sins. He was willing to be crucified, knowing that He would rise from the dead. He is now in Heaven, still waiting God's *time* to make Him king on earth.

Happy are the meek—those who wait patiently for God.

Day 11   Read Matthew 5:5

Hide and Seek Words ☐
As you read your Bible try to find these hidden words:

"...but the meek shall inherit the earth"

A Special Inheritance

Nancy was born in the city. She lived in the city. She went to school in the city. She attended church in the city. Almost all that Nancy knew about life outside the city was what she saw in a park.

One day Nancy, her mother and dad left that city house to spend a vacation with Mother's friend in the country.

"Why do carrots grow under the ground?" Nancy wanted to know. "Why don't they grow on trees like apples? I never knew you picked beans from a bush. I thought you just bought them in the store."

How surprised Nancy was to learn that almost all the food in cans and boxes had to first, in some way, come from the ground, or the earth. In this way God provides for our bodies. We patiently trust Him for these good things.

Remember, too, one day the meek (those who are waiting for the Lord Jesus) will rule the earth with Him. They shall inherit the earth.

Day 12   Read John 6:35

Hide and Seek Words ☐

As you read your Bible try to find these hidden words:

"Jesus said . . . I am the bread of life"

Bread from Heaven

When you eat and drink enough of the right food, your body has what it needs to grow. You are full, or satisfied. How hard people work to buy and prepare food for their bodies!

Did you know that your *soul* needs food, too? Just as your stomach gets an empty feeling when you are hungry, the real you (your soul) wants and needs something. You need to know and love and obey God.

The Lord Jesus said He is the "bread" or food for your soul. But there is something you must do. The promise is: He that *comes* and *believes* shall never hunger or thirst. You must take time to be with God in your Quiet Time and obey His words. Then He can satisfy your hungry soul!

At the end of Kathy's prayer one morning she said . . .

"Dear Jesus, help me to grow up with You!"

Be attitude 4

Day 13　　　　　　　　　　Read Psalm 42:1, 2

Hide and Seek Words ☐
As you read your Bible try to find these hidden words:
"My soul thirsteth for . . . the living God"

The Deer and the Brook

In the cool quietness of the woods, a water brook trickles over tiny pebbles. Suddenly a handsome deer (called a hart) dashes through the trees! He has been running for a long time. See, he is panting. He is so very, very thirsty. Down goes his nose into the cool, gurgling brook. He drinks and drinks some more. Then quick as a deer can go, he darts back into the woods. But he will be back!

Just as the hart (the deer) gets thirsty for water, your soul wants to know more and more about God. Stop right now and read Psalm 42:1 again.

Wonderful, wonderful Jesus!
Who can compare with Thee!
Wonderful, wonderful Jesus!
Fairer than all art Thou to me.
Wonderful, wonderful Jesus!
Oh, how my soul loves Thee!
Fairer than all the fairest,
Jesus, art Thou to me!

　　　　　　　　　Benjamin A. Baur

Day 14 Read Psalm 107:8, 9

Hide and Seek Words ☐
As you read your Bible try to find these hidden words:
"He fills the hungry soul with goodness"

Full-ish Debbie!

Debbie didn't eat any breakfast. And she only nibbled on the good lunch Mother made for her. She was thinking about the fair!

That afternoon Debbie ran to the fair with an empty stomach and a full purse. She bought cotton candy, popcorn, ice cream, chocolate fudge, peanuts, and soft pretzels! Debbie was really full. But it wasn't long before she had an awful ache inside.

Sometimes God's children try to satisfy their hungry souls with exciting music, sports, television programs, or traveling to beautiful places. These things are fun for awhile. But then there is an ache inside. Your soul is still hungry for God!

Let God fill your soul with *goodness*...

Talk with Him and read His book.
Go to Sunday school and Bible club.
Talk about the Lord Jesus with your friends.
Try to please God at all times.

God will keep His promise. Don't forget to thank Him for His goodness!

Day 15　　　　　　　　　　Read Ephesians 5:8, 9

Hide and Seek Words ☐
As you read your Bible try to find these hidden words:

"The fruit of the Spirit is ... righteousness"

It Can't Be Done!

Shawn told many boys and girls in his class about the Lord Jesus. He did not listen when they told dirty stories. He hardly ever got into a fight. He was always trying to help someone. In fact, Shawn was just the kind of Christian Scott wanted to be.

Now Scott really tried. But things didn't turn out right! Before he knew it, he was laughing at someone who was in trouble. He never seemed to be able to stop his fists from swinging when there was a fight. And bad words always popped out of his mouth before he could swallow them!

Can you guess why Scott was having such a hard time living for Jesus? He was trying to be like Shawn without any help. Righteousness (goodness) comes only from God, through His Holy Spirit. Scott was trying to be good by himself without praying and hiding God's word in his heart. IT CAN'T BE DONE!

Day 16 — Read Psalm 23:1-3

Hide and Seek Words ☐
As you read your Bible try to find these hidden words:

"He leadeth me in the paths of righteousness"

Goodness Pays!

There is no person who is righteous (all good) except God's own Son. He is called "Jesus Christ, the Righteous." He is the one who can help *you* to be good.

First, the Lord forgives your sin when you tell Him you have done wrong. He restores your soul (makes you right with God again). After Jesus forgives your sin, He helps you know how to please God. He leads you in the paths of righteousness—the right way.

Tony had received two warnings that he would be expelled from school if he caused any more trouble. Tony's Bible teacher prayed with him that God would make him a good student. "God did it, Daddy!" Tony told his father. His father visited the Bible teacher and showed her Tony's report card. On it were straight A's. Goodness pays!

Not everyone can get straight A's. But even more important, Tony wanted to do right.

Happy are they who want to please God.

Day 17   Read Psalm 89:1

Hide and Seek Words ☐
As you read your Bible try to find these hidden words:
"I will sing of the mercies of the Lord"

Be Happy

The word "mercy" means "not to punish someone when he deserves it and to show him love." The "merciful" are those people who are "full of mercy." They forgive others and are kind to them—even if they don't deserve it!

Sin must be punished. God lets the Lord Jesus take your punishment for doing wrong. This is why He can be merciful to you! He can forgive you and show love to you by giving you all you need.

If you are really thankful for God's mercy, your happy heart will tell your mouth about it, and your mouth will tell your friends and family!

Think of God's great mercy;
Be prayerful and still.
To be thankful and happy
Surely is His will.

Be attitude 5

Day 18   Read Ephesians 4:32

Hide and Seek Words ☐

As you read your Bible try to find these hidden words:

"Be ye kind ... forgiving one another"

Jesus Shows Us

It was night. Jesus prayed in the garden. His disciples fell asleep. Leaders and guards came. Judas betrayed Him with a kiss. The disciples ran away into the night. The guards bound Jesus and led Him away. They mocked Him and spit upon Him. They beat Him. Finally they led Him through the streets. He carried a cross upon His shoulders. The crowds gathered to mock and laugh. Outside the city walls on a hill they crucified Him. Jesus' first words from that cross were a prayer: "Father, forgive them, for they know not what they do."

Jesus was asking forgiveness for:

    Those who nailed Him to the cross.

    Those who mocked and laughed.

    Those leaders who planned His crucifixion.

    Those who ran away when He needed them.

If I am merciful I, too, forgive:

    those who hit or hurt me.

    Those who make fun because I am a Christian.

    Those who do not like me.

    Those who disappoint me.

Day 19　　　　　　　　　　Read Luke 6:35, 36

Hide and Seek Words □

As you read your Bible try to find these hidden words:

"Be ye therefore merciful"

God Says So!

One day Stephen asked, "Do Christians like other Christians?" This sounds like a funny question, but it is a good one. One of Stephen's Christian friends had made him feel that he didn't like him.

Sometimes we forget how kind God is to us and think we can treat others any way we want. God says we are to forgive others and be kind to everyone. But we should be *extra* nice to those who belong to the Lord Jesus. It hurts Him when we aren't.

Remember, a merciful boy or girl is one who does not act mean toward someone—even when he deserves it! He shows kindness. Jesus' power can help you do this. Then you will have the happiness that comes to those who are full of mercy.

THINK ABOUT THIS:

A mean word is always heard by God!

Day 20   Read Psalm 18:25

Hide and Seek Words ☐
As you read your Bible try to find these hidden words:
"Thou wilt show thyself merciful"

No End!

Here is some "Bible Science." God's kindness to you causes you to want to be kind. Your kindness to others causes more kindness to you from God.

So, you see, it goes on and on. God's mercy to us never runs out. One day we will understand even more how merciful God has been to us.

The Judgment

Some day, after all my play,
Work and years and days,
I will live with God in Heav'n
Singing all His praise.

God is judge upon the throne.
My whole life I'll see,
All that's good and all that's bad
Tears will surely be!

Mercy I will feel anew
When Christ speaks for me.
Help me, Lord, here on earth
Now to speak for Thee.

Day 21　　　　　　　　　Read 1 John 1:6, 7

Hide and Seek Words ☐
As you read your Bible try to find these hidden words:

**"The blood of Jesus Christ...
cleanseth us from all sin"**

The Aspirin

"Mother, Mother," shouted Tommy as he came running into the house. "Quick, give me an aspirin. The girls are bothering me and I want to take an aspirin!" The TV commercial had convinced Tommy that aspirin could do anything.

Tommy thought that something man had made could solve or take away a problem he had with people and himself.

God's Word says nothing man has made or can do is able to solve the problem of getting rid of our sin. Believing that Jesus died on the cross and rose again for your sins, receiving Him as your Savior, is the only way to be made clean (pure).

Have you told the Lord Jesus you believe this and received Him as your Savior?

> What can wash away my sin?
> 　　Nothing but the blood of Jesus.

Be attitude 6

Day 22   Read Psalm 24:3-5

Hide and Seek Words ☐
As you read your Bible try to find these hidden words:

"He that hath...a pure heart"

Stolen Dimes

Rachel sneaked ever so quietly into her parents' room and carefully opened the heavy dresser drawer. She took the lid off the dime bank and jingled several dimes into her hand. Putting the bank back in place, she closed the drawer...just in time.

At the store after school, those same dimes were handed to the owner for a chocolate-marshmallow ice cream cone. Oh, how good it was! This happened again and again and again!

Many years later Rachel received the Lord Jesus as her Savior. She knew He forgave her for stealing the dimes. She wanted to please the Lord Jesus. She even showed her parents that she had a pure heart by confessing to them her sin of stealing.

Are you looking forward to seeing the Lord Jesus? God's promise, "The pure in heart...*shall* see God."

Day 23   Read 1 Timothy 4:12 and 5:22

Hide and Seek Words ☐
As you read your Bible try to find these hidden words:

**"Neither be partaker of
other men's sins"**

A Sad Story

God means for each of us to be ourselves and not a copy of someone else. But it is easy to do what our friends say so they will like us or not make fun of us.

Twelve-year-old Jeremy always wanted to lead the prayer time at Bible club. He did a good job of it. One day the teacher learned something sad. Jeremy often got in trouble with boys on the school bus and refused to obey the driver when he told him to behave. Jeremy took part in the other boys' sin. The bus driver and the other children saw he was not a good example. The bus driver just laughed at Jeremy when he went to Bible club, saying it didn't do him any good.

Though Jeremy was a Christian, he did not keep himself pure.

Do others see Jesus in me?

Am I an example, Lord, for You?

Day 24   Read Luke 2:11-14

Hide and Seek Words ☐

As you read your Bible try to find these hidden words:

"On earth peace, good will toward men"

The Peacemaker from Heaven

To have peace is to be friendly with someone or agree with him. The Bible tells us that no one is born with peace in his heart toward God. All are unfriendly toward Him. We have wanted our own way. This is sin! Because God loves us He sent a peacemaker from Heaven.

The Lord Jesus is the peacemaker sent from God. Angels shouted the news across the sky: "On earth peace!" Although Jesus was only a baby when the angels shouted "Peace," they knew He would never do anything wrong. He would die for the sins of us all so that we could be forgiven and have peace with God.

Have you believed that Jesus died and rose again for your sin? If you have truly believed on Him, you do not want to go your own way. You are His friend. The Lord Jesus once said, "You are my friends, if you do whatsoever I command you."

BE attitude 7

Day 25   Read John 20:19-21

Hide and Seek Words ☐

As you read your Bible try to find these hidden words:

"... so send I you"

A Mission for You!

Jesus, the peacemaker, gave special instructions to His disciples: "As my Father hath sent me, even so send I you." The disciples were to be peacemakers, too!

How were they to carry out their new job? They would tell others how to have their sins forgiven. By believing on the Lord Jesus, these people would have peace with God. What an exciting mission!

Peter had his watch stolen by his best friend, Nick. Peter did not want to tell on his friend. Instead Peter told Nick how the Lord Jesus died for sin. "Wait a minute until I run home," said Nick. Soon he returned... with the watch!

If you belong to the Lord Jesus, your mission is to be a peacemaker. For He says, "So send I YOU."

    I want to serve Jesus, don't you?

    I want to be faithful and true;

    To tell the glad story, live for His glory,

    And hear His "Well done," don't you?

Day 26   Read Ephesians 6:1-3

Hide and Seek Words ☐

As you read your Bible try to find these hidden words:

"Children, obey your parents in the Lord"

Peacemakers at Home

Kevin's father was building a house two miles from home. Mother said "No" when Kevin asked if he could go and watch. When Mother was not watching him Kevin ran down the road to see his father. Kevin did not get lost or hurt, but his father and mother were very disappointed that he had not obeyed.

God has given you parents to help you grow up. When you learn to obey them it is much easier to obey God. He wants you to be a peacemaker in your home. You can do this by obeying your parents.

Write some ways that you can be a peacemaker at your house:

I will _____

_____

_____

Day 27   Read Romans 14:19

Hide and Seek Words □

As you read your Bible try to find these hidden words:

**"Follow after the things
that make for peace"**

Peacemakers at Play

Emily, Anna and Kristen were playing together and having lots of fun. Soon Emily and Anna began to whisper secrets. They did not include Kristen in the fun. Kristen went home, sat down on her front steps and began to pout. The next time they played together, Kristen tried to get back at her friends by telling Emily secrets and not allowing Anna to hear. How could Kristen have been a peacemaker?

God allows trouble in our lives so that we can learn how to be peacemakers. Here are three steps to follow that "make for peace:"

1. Thank God for the problem.
2. Find out what caused it.
3. Ask the Lord what He wants
   you to learn from this problem.

Memorize these steps and use them when trouble comes. You can be a peacemaker; and others will see that you are a child of God!

Day 28   Read Matthew 5:10

Hide and Seek Words ☐
As you read your Bible try to find these hidden words:
"...**persecuted for righteousness' sake**"

You Can Expect It!

Can you be happy when someone makes fun of you for doing good? God says you can be! To be persecuted means to be treated badly. It is hard to be treated badly for doing right.

When the Lord Jesus was here on earth He always did good. But many people persecuted *Him*. Finally they even put Him to death. Why did they do it? His goodness made their sin look even worse! They hated Him for this. And so Jesus warned His disciples, "If the world [people who do not love God] hate you, you know that it hated me before it hated you.... If they have persecuted me, they will also persecute you..." (John 15:18, 20). Yes, you can expect it to happen!

The same day the Lord Jesus spoke the Beatitudes, He said we should pray for the happiness of those who speak evil about us (Luke 6:28).

BE attitude 8

Day 29   Read 1 Thessalonians 5:24

Hide and Seek Words ☐
As you read your Bible try to find these hidden words:
"Faithful is he that calleth you"

A Faithful Friend

Caroline's friend Robyn helped her in knowing how to receive the Lord Jesus one day after Bible club. Happily, Caroline skipped home and told her mother that she had received the Lord Jesus as her Savior from sin. But her mother was angry!

"Caroline, I forbid you to go to the club again! And you are not to be friends with any of the boys and girls who attend that club or go to church!"

Caroline obeyed her mother. She never again mentioned receiving the Lord Jesus but she knew He was living in her. When Caroline grew up God helped her study to be a missionary doctor.

When you have a hard time living for Jesus, remember that He is faithful—He will not let you down! Write your Hide and Seek Words

here:_____

_____

Thank God for this wonderful promise.

Day 30 Read Matthew 5:11, 12

Hide and Seek Words ☐
As you read your Bible try to find these hidden words:

"...great is your reward in heaven"

Happy Day!
There's a mansion in Heaven
Awaiting for me

David's eyes sparkled. "You say you have a mansion in Heaven?" he questioned as he looked at the teacher who had just finished singing the song.

"Oh, yes, I do," she answered. "But you may have one, too."

Together they studied the words of the Lord Jesus who said, "Let not your heart be troubled...in my Father's house [Heaven] are many mansions [homes, rooms, dwelling places]..."(John 14:1-3).

That day David asked the Lord Jesus to be his Savior from sin, and now he too can sing...

There's a mansion in Heaven
Awaiting for me.

When trouble comes, think of that happy day in Heaven. Troubles last for awhile, but Heaven will be for ever and ever and ever!

It's Sure Hard to Believe You're a Christian

Day 1 — Read Isaiah 59:2

Hide and Seek Words ☐

As you read your Bible try to find these hidden words:

"Your iniquities [sins] have separated . . . you and . . . God"

How God Feels About Sin

God is holy—without sin. He tells us in the Bible that there can be no sin where He is. He cannot even stand to look at sin! This is why people are separated from God. For everyone on this earth has sinned—thought, and said, and done bad things.

Sometimes people talk about *little* sins, like a "little white lie." They don't understand how God feels about sin. Every sin is terrible to Him because it is like a wall that comes between you and God. God loves you. He wants you to be His child. He wants you never to be separated from Him again.

God hates sin so much that He sent His only dear Son, the Lord Jesus, to take all the punishment for all sin. Jesus Christ died for *your* sin!

Do you believe Jesus died for you? Tell Him so today!

Day 2 — Read Colossians 1:14

Hide and Seek Words ☐
As you read your Bible try to find these hidden words:

"... through his [Jesus'] blood ... the forgiveness of sin"

God Makes the Rules

Susan had received the Lord Jesus as her Savior—she was a Christian. She told her friend Mrs. Turner about the Lord Jesus. "He will forgive all your sins, if you ask Him to."

"But I am not a sinner, Susan. There is no such thing as sin. You see, it's like this. You and I and everyone in this world are traveling toward the top of the hill (Heaven). You walk on one side of the hill and I walk on the other side. But when we reach the top, we will both have the same view!"

There were tears in Susan's eyes. "Mrs. Turner, I don't like to say this, but God's Word says if you do not believe Jesus died for you and trust Him, you will never see Heaven."

Someone had taught Mrs. Turner the wrong way. She had not listened to God's Word. And it is God who makes the rules!

Jesus said, "I am the way ... no man cometh ... but by me" (John 14:6).

Day 3   Read Isaiah 53:6

Hide and Seek Words ☐

As you read your Bible try to find these hidden words:

"The Lord hath laid on him the iniquity of us all"

It Has to Go Somewhere!

Even though God loves us, He could not overlook sin or forget it.

If I have a book in my hand and want to lay it down, I must lay it on a table or on a chair, or on the floor, or on *something*. I cannot lay it "nowhere"! God knew there was nothing we could do with our sins and so He placed them on His own Son. When Jesus died on the cross, He was taking the punishment for your sin and mine.

Because the Lord Jesus took the punishment you deserved, God can now forget your sin. When you call on God and believe on the Lord Jesus, your sins are forgiven. He blots out your transgressions (your sins) and they are never seen again!

"As far as the east is from the west, so far hath he removed our transgressions from us" (Psalm 103:12).

Day 4 Read John 5:24

Hide and Seek Words ☐
As you read your Bible try to find these hidden words:

"He that...believeth...shall not come into condemnation"

Guilty or Not Guilty?

A man stepped before the judge. He had broken the law. "Guilty," cried the judge. "Your sentence is death." The man was under *condemnation*. This means he was guilty and waiting to be punished.

God says that all who do not believe on Him are under condemnation. They are guilty of sin (breaking God's laws). They will have to be separated from Him forever.

But those who believe that Jesus died in their place will NOT come into condemnation. The very moment you believe on the Lord Jesus, God can say to you, "Not guilty." You will never have to be separated from God. You receive everlasting *life*.

> What a great salvation,
> Now *no condemnation,*
> Praise His Name
> There's no separation
> When God takes hold!

Day 5   Read 2 Corinthians 5:15

Hide and Seek Words ☐
As you read your Bible try to find these hidden words:

"... should not ... live unto themselves, but unto him"

A True Christian

If you have received the Lord Jesus as your Savior from sin, you have everlasting life. Now, can you do just as you please? NO! God says you should not keep on sinning. The Lord Jesus died to set you free from the power of sin. He did this so that you could stop living for yourself and live for Him.

God wants you to be more and more like His Son every day. What was the Lord Jesus like? In Hebrews 1:9 it says He "loved righteousness [goodness] and *hated* iniquity [sin]!" Ask the Lord Jesus to help you turn away from sin and do good. Remember how much God loves you and wants to show His love through you as you obey Him.

Carlos, who lives in Chile, said, "I want to be a Christian like Salvador. He doesn't lie or say bad words, and he eats all his food!"

If you love God, you will want to do the things He tells you to do.

Day 6   Read 1 John 1:8

Hide and Seek Words ☐

As you read your Bible try to find these hidden words:

"If we say that we have no sin we deceive [lie to] ourselves"

Does a Christian Sin?

When you received the Lord Jesus as your Savior, did you think you would never sin again? What do the Hide and Seek Words say about this?

One day after Sunday school two boys came to the teacher. One said, "Joe and I don't know whether we are still Christians."

"Have you received the Lord Jesus as your Savior from sin?" the teacher asked. They both said they had. "Then why do you think you are not saved?"

"Well," Jason answered, "we tell lies sometimes."

The teacher explained, "When you do something wrong at home you still belong to your mother and dad. But they are sad because you have been naughty. When you received the Lord Jesus, you were born into God's family. You will always belong to Him. But it grieves Him (makes Him sad) when you sin. Tell Him you are sorry. He promises to forgive you!"

Day 7   Read Matthew 26:40, 41

Hide and Seek Words ☐

As you read your Bible try to find these hidden words:

**"... the spirit ... is willing
... the flesh is weak"**

Why Does a Christian Sin?

A Christian should not sin. He does not want to grieve God. But he sometimes does!

Did you ever feel as though you were two people inside instead of one, and that the two people were fighting each other? When you become a Christian it is something like that. Suppose you see a nice red ball that belongs to your neighbor. Something inside you says, "He's not around; take it home." Another something inside says, "Don't take that ball; that's stealing." "But no one will ever know you took it." "God will know." "Take it." "Don't." There is a real fight going on! This is because there is a new "you" that wants to please the Lord Jesus, but the old "you" is still there and wants his own way.

If you take the ball, you are saying "Yes" to the old "you." But God says, "...sin shall not have dominion over you..." which means *sin shall not be your master*. Let the new "you" be in control—say "No" to sin. Thank the Lord Jesus that though you are weak, He is strong.

Day 8   Read 1 Peter 5:8

Hide and Seek Words □

As you read your Bible try to find these hidden words:

"... your adversary [your enemy] the devil"

Your Enemy

Sometimes you may wonder why it is so hard to live for the Lord Jesus and do the things that please Him. Have you forgotten that you have an enemy?

Satan knows that if he can get you to sin, he may keep you from helping others find the way to Heaven! Satan is like a lion, sneaking around, trying to catch someone in the jaws of sin!

Jim had only been a Christian for a week. He started down the street one day when another boy came from behind and gave him a push. At first Jim paid no attention, but the boy kept trying to make him fight. At last Jim turned to him and said, "I used to fight, but I can't fight with you, because I'm a Christian now."

Satan may try to make trouble for you through other people. Trust God to give you the victory over Satan. Look in 1 John 4:4 for God's promise.

Look out for Satan

Day 9   Read Romans 6:16

Hide and Seek Words ☐

As you read your Bible try to find these hidden words:

". . . his servants ye are to whom ye obey"

It's Your Choice!

Two boys were arguing about a chair. Steve said to the teacher, "John took my chair. I had my jacket and books on it and he moved them."

The teacher asked John to move over, but he said, "No." Then she asked him if he knew he was not pleasing the Lord Jesus. John looked down but did not answer. He refused to obey.

As John sat there the Holy Spirit spoke to him through our Hide and Seek Words, for he was a Christian. Looking up with a smile, John moved to the next chair.

You can choose to do the right or the wrong thing. If you really want to be God's servant (to obey Him), you will even be willing to give up what belongs to you. Do you know what happens when you yield (say "yes") to the Lord? You have a special joy and peace in your heart!

Day 10   Read Ephesians 5:15-17

Hide and Seek Words ☐

As you read your Bible try to find these hidden words:

"**... walk circumspectly
... wise ... because the days are evil**"

Be Wise!

A Christian may sin because he becomes careless.

To "walk circumspectly" (sir-come-spect-lee) is "to be careful how you act." There is a lot of sin in the world around you. A wise Christian is careful, for it is easy to get trapped in sin.

Two children were sent to take some cookies to an old lady who was sick. On the way they opened the basket and counted the cookies. "Let's share a cookie. I don't believe one would be missed," said Jackie.

"Oh, yes it would," replied Tami. "Don't you know that God can count?"

We must be careful to follow our friends only when they obey God!

Dear Father, each day as I work and play,
Help me to use my ears and eyes—
To know what is wrong and turn away
Then I'll be a Christian who's wise!

Day 11   Read James 1:5, 6

Hide and Seek Words ☐

As you read your Bible try to find these hidden words:

"...ask in faith"

Faith Is a Must!

Did you ever say, "Well, I prayed for something, but my prayer wasn't answered"? The Bible says, "...ask in faith...." What is faith? It is just believing what God says is true, and that He will do it.

God has promised that sin shall not have dominion over you (Romans 6:14). This means that sin shall not rule or get the best of you. Is there some sin that you keep giving in to? And you have tried and tried not to do that wrong thing over again? Maybe you have prayed and asked the Lord to help you, but you still can't stop it.

Are you asking in faith? Do you really believe that God is going to help you? Keep on praying. God *will* do it!

"...all things are possible to him that believeth" (Mark 9:23).

Ask in faith

Day 12   Read Psalm 119:11, 12

Hide and Seek Words ☐
As you read your Bible try to find these hidden words:

"Thy word have I hid in mine heart"

Use the Sharp One!

God says that His Word, the Bible, is our weapon against sin. And it is *sharper* than any two-edged sword! (Hebrews 4:12)

A teacher once asked her class, "Why should you hide Bible verses in your heart by memorizing them?"

Randy's hand shot up first. "So when I need them, I have them!"

Some Christians have trouble with sin because they don't memorize God's Word. They don't have their sharp weapon when they need it. Do you?

Write here a verse that you will memorize today:

_____

_____

_____

_____

Day 13   Read Hebrews 13:5, 6

Hide and Seek Words ☐
As you read your Bible try to find these hidden words:
"I will *never* leave thee"

What Is Lost?

When you sin will you lose everlasting life and have to receive the Lord Jesus as Savior again? Find the words of Jesus in John 10:28 and write the answer (yes or no) here. _____ If you are not sure your answer is right, look at the Hide and Seek Words again.

Eternal or everlasting life does last forever! It cannot be taken away from those who believe the Lord Jesus died for them and ask Him to forgive their sin. But there are some things that a Christian *can* lose when he does wrong. For the next few days we are going to think about the ways that sin hurts a Christian.

Be sure not to miss your Quiet Time one single day. You will not want to lose *any* of these things!

Day 14   Read 1 John 1:5-7

Hide and Seek Words ☐

As you read your Bible try to find these hidden words:

**"If we walk in the light
... we have fellowship"**

Lost... Fellowship!

To have fellowship with God is to feel friendly toward Him. Fellowship is to be able to talk with Him and know that He is pleased with you.

Darkness and light cannot be together. If a room is all dark, it is because the light has been put out. If a room is lit up, the darkness has gone.

The Bible says that darkness reminds us of *sin* and light makes us think of *no sin*. And so, God is sometimes called light. He is without sin—"in him is no darkness at all."

If you say that you are getting along all right with God (having fellowship with Him) and are allowing sin in your life, you are lying! Tell God you are sorry for your sin. He will forgive you, and you will be close friends again.

Day 15   Read Psalm 51:10, 12

Hide and Seek Words ☐

As you read your Bible try to find these hidden words:

"Restore [return] unto me the joy of thy salvation"

Lost...Joy!

"Dear Lord Jesus, whatever would I do without You? I thank You many thousand times that you came into my heart," Freddie prayed one day.

Do you remember how full of joy you were when you asked Jesus to be your Savior? When you sin, you lose that wonderful joy. You become troubled because you know that God is displeased. But when you talk to God about that sin and ask Him to help you stop it, the joy will return!

Is there some sin you need to talk to God about?

Nothing between my soul and the Savior,
So that His blessed face may be seen;
Nothing preventing the least of His favor,
Keep the way clear, let nothing between.

—Tingley

Day 16

Read John 15:4, 5

Hide and Seek Words ☐

As you read your Bible try to find these hidden words:

[Jesus said], "Without me ye can do nothing"

Lost...Power!

If you would pull a branch from a grapevine, what would happen to it? If you kept the branch, would you be able to get grapes from it? Why not? These answers are very easy. The branch gets its power to give grapes from the vine. Without the vine the branch has lost its power!

Jesus said that *He* is like the vine and *you* are like a branch. When you abide in (stay close friends with) the Lord Jesus, many good things come from your life. You are like a branch that gives fruit! But when there is sin in your life, you are not abiding in Jesus (you are not close friends with Him). Without abiding in the Lord Jesus you have lost your power to please God. You can do NOTHING for God until you ask Him to forgive that sin.

But with Him I can do all things,
With Him vict'ry is mine;
With Him I shall be fruitful—
I'm the branch and He's the Vine.

Day 17   Read 2 Corinthians 5:10

Hide and Seek Words □

As you read your Bible try to find these hidden words:

"**. . . every one may receive
. . . that he hath done**"

Lost . . . Rewards!

Everlasting life is a free *gift*. You cannot work for it and earn it, for the Lord Jesus has already paid for it. You may only believe and take it!

If you have received God's gift, you will then want to work for Him because you love Him, and because you know it pleases Him. He set you free from sin so that you could do good works.

One day, after the Lord Jesus comes back, every Christian will stand before Him. He will look over all the things you have done—the good and the bad. For the good things you have done, you will receive special rewards. But for the bad things, you will lose rewards. They will be lost forever.

Ask God each day to help you keep sin out of your life, so there will be no lost rewards!

> A crown to win, a crown to win,
> A crown each boy and girl may win.
> We've entered in, we're cleansed from sin,
> Now by His help a crown we'll win.

Day 18   Read Hebrews 12:5, 6

Hide and Seek Words ☐

As you read your Bible try to find these hidden words:

"... whom the Lord loveth he chasteneth [punishes]"

Punishment Helps!

"You don't have to spank me anymore," Jan said to Mother after Sunday school. "Jesus took the punishment for my sin." Jan was *right* ... and *wrong!*

Jesus did take the punishment for your sin. But when you received the Lord Jesus, you became part of God's family. Now, when you do wrong, God punishes you because He loves you!

How does God's punishment show that He loves you? He knows that the wrong things you do will bring unhappiness to you here on earth. He does not want you to lose fellowship, joy, power, and rewards. And so your Heavenly Father chastens (punishes) you when you sin to *help* you stop it! When you are young, He often lets your mother and father do this for Him. When they punish you for doing wrong, they show that they love you, too.

Day 19　　　　　　　　　　Read Ephesians 4:25

Hide and Seek Words ☐
As you read your Bible try to find these hidden words:

"... speak every man truth"

Scars

Peblos had a very bad habit of telling lies—but he didn't see how they hurt anyone! One day the missionary gave him a hammer and nails. "Peblos," he said, "see that post? Every time you tell an untruth, I want you to hammer a nail into the post."

It was not long before Peblos was telling a whole "string" of lies. The next day he was feeling very guilty. He hammered and hammered until there was a nail in the post for each lie.

When the missionary saw the nails he was glad that Peblos admitted his sin. He prayed with him and Peblos asked forgiveness. Then the missionary helped Peblos pull out every nail. The post was full of holes! "Yes, Peblos," the missionary said, "the Lord has forgiven your sin, but sin leaves scars in your life. Remember, it is better *not* to sin in the first place."

Day 20   Read 1 John 2:1

Hide and Seek Words ☐

As you read your Bible try to find these hidden words:

"... we have an advocate ... Jesus Christ"

He's Praying for You

Over and over again in God's Word He promises to hear and answer your prayers. But did you know that sin can block your prayers? It could be disobeying, pouting, lying, or cheating. With sin in your life, you cannot expect God to answer your prayers. As God's child, you need to confess your sin when you have done something wrong. Your Hide and Seek Words promise that the Lord Jesus who lives in Heaven is your advocate—the one who pleads for you before your Heavenly Father. He can be depended upon to forgive you and make you clean from all sin. Thank Him that He prays for you. Thank Him that as you confess your sin, He removes the sin blocking your prayers.

Jesus prays for you

Day 21   Read 1 Corinthians 15:57

Hide and Seek Words ☐

As you read your Bible try to find these hidden words:

"... the victory through our Lord Jesus Christ"

Battle Plans

Captain Owens knew the enemy was near. It was time for his soldiers to carry out the plans he had given them. Each soldier was in his place. The signal was given. Every order was obeyed, and the battle was won!

The Lord Jesus saved us from the penalty of sin. One day He will come and take us to Heaven where there is no sin. But right now, here on earth, He said we will have to fight sin. Jesus is our captain. He gives us the battle plans in *the Bible,* and the power to win through *His Holy Spirit.*

Jesus is the greatest captain of all, for He arose from the dead. He is alive. He had victory over sin and death! Will you follow the orders of your captain? You can count on Him to give *you* victory, too.

Day 22　　　　　　　　　　Read Philippians 4:13

Hide and Seek Words ☐
As you read your Bible try to find these hidden words:
"I can ... through Christ"

Stay in Your Seat

"David is doing well in all his subjects," the teacher reported at parent-teacher conference. "But he just can't stay in his seat. He is always talking with the other children."

David tried, but he just couldn't! He was punished. "I'm sorry, Mother," he said, "but I can't."

"Did you know there is a verse in the Bible which says you can stay in your seat?" she asked. David was surprised. Mother opened her Bible to Philippians 4:13 and read, "I can do all things [stay in my seat] through Christ which strengtheneth me." David printed the words on a card which he placed on his desk. "I can," he called, as he returned from school. "The Lord Jesus gives me strength to do what I cannot do alone!"

Day 23   Read 1 John 1:9

Hide and Seek Words ☐

As you read your Bible try to find these hidden words:

"...he is faithful...to forgive us"

Order: Confess!

Kelly and Joy Ann were best friends. They played with each other all the time. One day they got into a fight over Joy Ann's new bicycle. Later that day Kelly felt sad. She wanted to go to Joy Ann and say she was sorry, but she was afraid Joy Ann would not forgive her.

Do you know when the best time is to confess (tell) your sin to the Lord Jesus? As soon as you know that you have done wrong! You don't have to be afraid that God will not forgive you. He promises to forgive you right away, no matter what the sin may be. This is why He gave His life's blood on the cross—to cleanse you from *all* sin (unrighteousness).

To confess your sin also means to be sorry for it. When you tell your sin to the Lord Jesus, ask Him to help you not to do it again.

Day 24   Read Proverbs 28:13

Hide and Seek Words ☐
As you read your Bible try to find these hidden words:
"He that covereth his sins shall not prosper"

Order: Confess!

When Zacchaeus believed in Jesus as his Savior, he remembered the people from whom he had stolen money. Before he could have real peace in his heart he had to repay each person (Luke 19:1-10).

Tara wanted to prove to her two friends that she was not afraid to do anything, and so she stole some barrettes from the store. After she received the Lord Jesus as Savior and let Him take control of her life, she knew that she had to go back to this store and tell what she had done. She took her own money and paid for the barrettes she had stolen. It was not an easy thing to do. But afterwards God filled her heart with His peace. Tara had a real victory over sin!

Is there something in your life that has never been made right? Why not take care of it now! God will give you the courage.

Day 25　　　　　　　　　　Read Hebrews 12:1

Hide and Seek Words ☐

As you read your Bible try to find these hidden words:

"... let us lay aside ... sin"

Order: Leave Sin Behind!

Daniel's friends called him to come and join in their race. Ten boys were going to race the length of the playground. First Daniel laid down the package he was carrying. After that he emptied all his pockets, so that *nothing* would slow him down. Then he was ready to do his best!

The Christian life is like a race. You must lay aside anything that would keep you from doing your best. The Bible calls these things "weights" and "sin." Each one of us has sin which we must lay aside or stay away from, if we are to follow Jesus. It may be lying, cheating, bragging, swearing, or stealing. Perhaps you have a secret sin no on knows about. If you want your life to count for God, you must lay aside *all* sin. Look to Jesus, your captain. He will help you!

THINK ABOUT THIS:
Something good can be a "weight" if it keeps me from my Quiet Time.

Day 26   Read Philippians 3:13, 14

Hide and Seek Words ☐

As you read your Bible try to find these hidden words:

"... forgetting those things which are behind"

Order: Press On!

Tim was a great runner. He would always come in first in a race. Tim was a winner not only because he was fast, but because he knew a secret that all good runners know: NEVER LOOK BEHIND. When a runner looks behind he loses time and may lose the race. Tim would set his eyes on the goal ahead, then run with all his might.

Again, we see that the Christian life is like a race. We are the runners. The prize is our reward in Heaven.

In this race of life, many times we fail to trust God; we sin. When we ask the Lord Jesus to forgive us, we go on in the race, forgetting what is behind. When sin is forgiven, God forgets it, and so we can forget it, too! Satan keeps trying to remind us of past sin to make us unhappy.

Day 27

Read Ephesians 6:16

Hide and Seek Words ☐

As you read your Bible try to find these hidden words:

"Above all, taking the shield of faith"

Order: Have Faith

What is a shield? (A shield is something that covers or protects us from harm.)

What is faith? Let me tell you about Sam. Sam walked into the newspaper office to ask if he could get a job as a newsboy. He gave the man behind the desk a note that had been written by his minister. On the paper was Sam's name and one line: "You can depend on anything he tells you." Sam's minister had faith in him. He knew Sam could be depended upon—he would not lie.

In your fight against sin, you must have faith in God. You can depend on His promises, for God cannot lie. Your faith in Him is like a shield. It stops (quenches) the fiery darts of Satan!

Day 28   Read James 4:7

Hide and Seek Words □
As you read your Bible try to find these hidden words:

"Resist the devil, and he will flee [run]"

Order: Resist!

Tom always tried to be a good Christian and obey his parents. But every time he played with Ben, he would get into trouble. Then his mother would punish him. After this happened many times, Tom asked the Lord to help him say "No" to Ben and do what was right.

Satan is really the one who wants you to sin. He will even use your friends to trick you and get you to do wrong. You need to submit or say "Yes" to God, and resist or say "No" to Satan. As you obey the Lord Jesus, He can make you wise to Satan's tricks.

When the Lord Jesus was tempted to sin, He ordered Satan away by saying, "Get thee behind me, Satan, for it is written...." Then Jesus quoted God's Word the Bible. When Satan tempts you to sin, you can use God's Word, too. The Bible is called the sword of the Spirit (Ephesians 6:17).

Day 29   Read 2 Timothy 2:22

Hide and Seek Words ☐
As you read your Bible try to find these hidden words:
"Flee also youthful lusts"

Order: Run!

Sometimes God wants you to stand still and say "No" to Satan, and sometimes He wants you to run away from sin!

Carla and Lindsay were on a picnic. They were finishing their lunch when suddenly Carla saw a bear. It was hungry and they had food. Carla and Lindsay did not wait one minute. They ran as fast as they could to the car. This is what it means to flee!

There are things you may be tempted to do wrong. The Lord Jesus says to run from these sins. One temptation to run away from is stealing. Another is smoking, which can harm your body. Run away from people who offer you pills and drugs. Unless drugs come from your parents or your doctor, they can cause terrible things to happen to you.

In your Bible verse today, you are told to follow with or make friends of those who love the Lord Jesus and are living to please Him.

Day 30
Read Revelation 22:20

Hide and Seek Words ☐

As you read your Bible try to find these hidden words:

"Even so, come, Lord Jesus"

Work While You Wait!

Coming for me, coming for me.
One day to earth He is coming for me.
Then with what joy His dear face I shall see.
Oh, how I praise Him! He's coming for me.

Can you make the Hide and Seek Words your prayer today? As you look forward to the return of the Lord Jesus, plan to keep busy each day doing the things you know He wants you to do. (Read James 4:17.)

1. Study God's Word (2 Timothy 2:15)

2. Talk to God in prayer (Philippians 4:6)

3. Obey your parents (Ephesians 6:1)

4. Love one another (1 John 3:23)

5. Do good unto all (Galatians 6:10)

6. Tell others about the Lord Jesus
   (2 Timothy 2:2)

We're Finding What God Wants Us to Do

Day 1   Read James 1:22

Hide and Seek Words ☐

As you read your Bible try to find these hidden words:

"...doers...and not hearers only"

All the Time

"You make me sick!" hissed Max as he jumped past his twin sister, Mindy, and ran down the church steps. Mindy's eyes filled with tears. "Why?" she asked. "Because you act so goody-goody in church and so awful at home," said Max. "Well!" snapped Mindy. "At least I'm not awful all the time like you."

The twins stopped at the bottom of the church steps and hung their heads in shame. "I'm sorry, Mindy," said Max. "Me, too," whispered Mindy. "But you know what?" said Max. "We're both right. We're great at going to church, but we're not so good at doing what we should the rest of the time." Mindy's eyes began to shine. "Max, let's really try to find out what God wants us to do and then do it." "Okay," agreed Max. "But all the time, not just on Sunday."

Day 2   Read James 4:8

Hide and Seek Words ☐

As you read your Bible try to find these hidden words:

"Draw nigh [near] to God, and he will draw nigh to you."

Near to God

"Okay, Mindy," said Max. "How are we going to get near to God so we can obey Him every day?"

Mindy thought and then said, "Well, we've both asked the Lord Jesus to come into our hearts and forgive the wrong things we've done. And we know we're going to Heaven when we die. I guess we'll just have to remember that He is with us every day."

Max grinned, "More like every minute. We sure can't live for Him by ourselves."

"We sure can't," echoed Mindy.

The twins both bowed their heads and Max prayed, "Lord Jesus, please help us to live for You every day and learn to obey You. Amen."

Max and Mindy looked at each other; a marvelous thing was happening to them. As they were trying to get near to God, God was coming near to them, just as He promised He would!

Day 3   Read Colossians 3:16

Hide and Seek Words ☐

As you read your Bible try to find these hidden words:

"Let the word of Christ dwell [live] in you richly"

Letting God's Word In

"What do you have there, Mindy?" asked Max.

Mindy showed Max a book. "It's a Bible with everything Jesus said marked in red. I told my Sunday school teacher that we wanted to try to obey the Lord Jesus all the time. She gave this Bible to me to read every day. She said that it would help me to know what to do to please God."

"That's great!" exclaimed Max. "I told my teacher, too, and he gave me a *Daily Bread for Girls & Boys*. I can read one page every day and then look up a verse in the Bible. I've started already and I'm really learning a lot."

"Me, too," said Mindy. "I've got an idea! When we find anything that tells us how to obey God, let's tell each other and then try to do it."

Max looked pleased. "That's a deal!"

Day 4   Read Colossians 3:17

Hide and Seek Words ☐
As you read your Bible try to find these hidden words:

"... do all in the name of the Lord"

How Do You Know?

"Max!" called Mindy. "I've found a verse in the Bible that tells us how to live every day for the Lord Jesus.

Max was surprised. "One verse tells you all of that?"

"Right!" exclaimed Mindy. "...whatsoever ye do in word or deed, do all in the name of the Lord...."

Max could hardly believe his ears. "Hey, that's good. Whatever you do in speaking or in acting, try to please God. Only, how do you know if you're pleasing Him?"

Mindy replied, "We're learning more about what God wants us to do as we study the Bible, but I think we can just ASK Him what to do too."

Max thought and then said, "It's all of that, but there's more. It's the way we feel about everything we do. Do we *want* God's or our own way?"

Day 5   Read 2 Peter 3:18

Hide and Seek Words ☐
As you read your Bible try to find these hidden words:

"... grow ... in the knowledge of our Lord"

Growing by Learning

"There's lots to learn about living for Jesus every day," sighed Max. "I thought it would be easy. We'd just have to act goody-goody all the time. But it's not like that at all!"

"Right!" said Mindy. "Jesus wants His people to be honest and not to pretend to be something they're not. He wants us to depend on Him to be what He wants us to be. He will help us obey everything He asks us to do; all we have to do is ask Him."

"We find out what God wants us to do by reading His Word and learning about Him, others, and ourselves," said Max.

"And then do what He tells us to!" exclaimed Mindy.

"That's the hard part," said Max. "That's where we've got to ask God for help 'cause we sure can't do it ourselves."

Day 6   Read Philippians 4:7

Hide and Seek Words ☐
As you read your Bible try to find these hidden words:

"...the peace of God...shall keep your hearts and minds"

Feeling Right

"Hey, Mindy!" called Max. "Do you feel different than you did before we started to try to live for God every day?"

"I sure do!" exclaimed Mindy. "I still get real mad and real sad and real glad, but there's something more now. It's sort of like feeling right with everything."

"Yes," said Max. "That's it. Right with everything."

Mindy thought for a minute. "I guess it's 'cause we know God is taking care of our lives and that He will NEVER let us down. He will NEVER stop loving us."

"That must be it," said Max. "Things aren't any easier; in fact, they sometimes get a lot harder when you try to live for the Lord Jesus. It's just that you know He is always there and everything feels exactly right."

Day 7   Read Philippians 4:6

Hide and Seek Words ☐
As you read your Bible try to find these hidden words:
"Let your requests [needs] be made known unto God"

Ask for Help

Mindy had a sad look on her pretty face. She sat thinking about the terrible book report she had to do. "I just hate to stand up in front of everyone... I know they will laugh at me... Max always makes faces at me... I just feel AWFUL!" She started to cry, "What am I going to do?"

Suddenly, a thought came to Mindy. *God says in His Word that He loves me and He wants me to tell Him all my problems so He can help.* Quickly, she bowed her head and whispered a prayer. "Lord Jesus, please help me with this book report. I'm so scared!" After a long time, she lifted her head and said, "Thank You, God. I know You'll help me. I just KNOW it!"

Day 8　　　　　　　　　　　Read 2 Timothy 2:7

Hide and Seek Words ☐
As you read your Bible try to find these hidden words:
"... the Lord give thee understanding"

Take It Easy!

Mindy threw the book on the floor. "I'll NEVER be able to give that old book report! I can't even understand what the book says, let alone tell anyone else about it." A tear ran down her cheek. She whispered, "Lord Jesus, please help me. I just can't get it."

Mindy stood up and walked over to the window. She got a kleenex to blow her nose. She felt calm as she sat down on the floor and picked up the book. Now, she thought, *I'll try it again.* She started reading the book and slowly she began to see what it was saying. "Oh, now I understand," she said as she read faster and faster. Before she knew it, the book was done. "Thank You, God," she prayed. "Thank You!"

Day 9   Read 1 Peter 5:7

Hide and Seek Words ☐

As you read your Bible try to find these hidden words:

"Casting [throwing] all your care upon him"

He Cares for You

"How come you're so happy today, Mindy?" asked Max. "Usually you bite my head off when you have to give a book report. What's wrong with you?"

"Well," replied Mindy, "Someone is helping me today."

"Really, who?" asked Max.

"The Lord Jesus," answered Mindy.

"Oh, come on," snorted Max. "How do you figure that?"

Mindy explained, "I asked Jesus to help me and I know He will. He promised He would in His Word and He loves me."

"We'll see about that when you stand up in front of everyone this morning in school," said Max as he ran out the front door.

Mindy picked up her books and then stopped and bowed her head. "Lord Jesus, I know You're going to help me 'cause You promised You would and 'cause I know You love me. Thank You."

Day 10   Read 2 Timothy 1:7

Hide and Seek Words ☐

As you read your Bible try to find these hidden words:

"... power and ... a sound mind"

Don't Be Afraid

Mindy's hands were sweaty as she held the book report in front of her. Her knees felt shaky and her stomach was jumping. She felt the eyes of everyone in her class on her. She looked at Max's grinning face. "Please help me, God," she prayed as she started to talk.

It was hard at first, but as she talked, it became easier until she looked up to see everyone listening to her. Suddenly, she wanted more than anything to explain to her friends exactly what the book said, and she forgot about being afraid.

In a few minutes she was all done. As she walked back to her seat she felt as if she was walking on air. God had answered her prayers just as He said He would.

Day 11   Read Philippians 4:13

Hide and Seek Words ☐
As you read your Bible try to find these hidden words:
"Christ...strengtheneth me"

I Can Do Anything!

"Mindy," called Max as he ran to catch up with her. "You did a great job on that book report. I could hardly believe it was you."

Mindy grinned shyly, "It wasn't me, Max; it was the Lord Jesus inside of me. I could never have done it alone. He did it through me."

"Wow!" said Max. "What did it feel like?"

Mindy thought for a long time and then said, "Really good! It was like, by myself I couldn't do anything, but with Jesus doing it through me, I could do anything...anything at all."

Day 12   Read Philippians 2:14

Hide and Seek Words ☐

As you read your Bible try to find these hidden words:

"... without murmurings [complaints] and disputings [arguments]"

Don't Complain and Argue

"Watch out, will you?" shouted Max as he jumped over Mindy, who was stretched out in front of the TV.

"What's the matter with you?" snapped Mindy.

"Nothing, except you're in my way and I don't like that program," snorted Max.

"Well, you're not going to change it," said Mindy in anger.

"You've seen that program three times already," insisted Max.

"I don't care; you're NOT going to change it!" yelled Mindy.

"Girls!" snarled Max. "Always got to have their own way."

"Look who has to have his own way!" screamed Mindy. There was a long silence as the children glared at each other.

"Boy!" said Max miserably, "we sure do sound like we're making God happy." Both stopped and asked the Lord's forgiveness quietly in their hearts.

Day 13

Read 1 John 4:11

Hide and Seek Words ☐

As you read your Bible try to find these hidden words:

"...love one another"

Love Each Other

"I'm sorry, Mindy," said Max softly.

"You always yell at me," pouted Mindy.

"I know I do," said Max, "and I shouldn't. The Lord Jesus tells us in the Bible that we should love each other because He loves us."

"He sure does," agreed Mindy. "He came down from Heaven to live here on earth as a man and died on the cross."

"Yes," said Max, "and He became alive again and went back to Heaven to get it ready for us to come and live with Him forever. All we have to do is believe Him and ask Him to come into our hearts and take away the wrong things we think and do."

Mindy sighed, "We've got a long way to go to love each other that much."

"We can try," suggested Max, "and anyway, He is here to help us!"

Day 14　　　　　　　　　Read Ephesians 4:32

Hide and Seek Words ☐

As you read your Bible try to find these hidden words:

"...kind...tenderhearted, forgiving"

Forgive Each Other

"Mindy, I want you to forgive me for getting mad at you," Max said.

Mindy cocked her head sideways. "You're really sorry, aren't you. I can hardly believe my ears," she giggled.

"Please don't laugh," said Max.

Mindy's pretty face became very serious. "Of course I'll forgive you, Max. But you'll have to forgive me 'cause I got mad right back at you."

"That's right, you did," agreed Max. "Okay, we'll make it go both ways. You forgive me and I'll forgive you."

"It's a deal!" said Mindy.

The twins grinned at each other. "It sure is nice to be friends again," said Max.

"Say, Max," teased Mindy, "let me turn on *your* program. I've watched this thing three times already." The two of them laughed and laughed.

Day 15   Read Galatians 6:2

Hide and Seek Words ☐
As you read your Bible try to find these hidden words:
"Bear ye one another's burdens"

Share Problems

"Max," said Mindy carefully. "Is there something else bothering you besides getting mad at me about the TV?"

"Yes, there is," said Max. "I'm having trouble with a kid at school."

"Who?" asked Mindy.

"A guy in my gym class named Chester. He's bad and he's always picking on me. It sure is hard to be nice to him as I know the Lord Jesus wants me to."

"I know that boy!" exclaimed Mindy. "He's a big bully! Oh, Max, no wonder you're upset. What has he done to you?"

"Lots of things," replied Max miserably.

"Tell me," said Mindy softly.

"Oh, it doesn't matter," said Max. "I wasn't going to say anything to anyone, but it sure feels good to be able to talk about it. Thanks, Mindy. You're okay, for a girl," he teased.

Day 16　　　　　　　　　　　Read Colossians 3:8

Hide and Seek Words ☐

As you read your Bible try to find these hidden words:

"... put off ... anger, wrath, malice [hate]"

Stop Hating!

"Max!" cried Mindy. "What happened to you?" Max came in the door and walked over to the kitchen sink. He took the cloth away from his bruised eye and turned on the cold water. "Did Chester do that to you?" asked Mindy as the tears welled up in her eyes. Max nodded his head yes. "Oh, that terrible person! I just HATE him!" cried Mindy.

"You can't," said Max in a muffled voice as he was wiping his face with a towel. "God told us in His Word that we're not supposed to hate anyone."

"Well," murmured Mindy. "He will just have to *help* us not to hate that awful Chester."

"That's right," said Max calmly. "*He* will have to help us not to hate."

Day 17   Read Ephesians 4:26

Hide and Seek Words ☐
As you read your Bible try to find these hidden words:
"Be ye angry, and sin not"

Stop Your Anger

"How do you feel, Max?" asked Mindy gently as she watched him get carefully into bed.

"My head hurts," said Max as he pulled the sheet up to his chin.

"What are you going to do about Chester hurting you?" asked Mindy as she turned out the light on the night stand.

"I've got to ask the Lord Jesus to help me stop being mad at him before I go to sleep tonight," replied Max as he put his hands behind his head.

"Guess I'll have to do the same thing," said Mindy as she walked out into the hallway, " 'cause I'm awful mad at him too." Quickly she walked into her bedroom and got on her knees and bowed her head. "Please, Lord Jesus, help me not to be angry at Chester for hurting Max."

Day 18　　　　　　　　　　Read Colossians 3:13

Hide and Seek Words □

As you read your Bible try to find these hidden words:

"... as Christ forgave you, so also do ye"

Forgive Him

Max listened to the clock ticking in the hallway as he lay in bed. His head hurt and he couldn't sleep. "God," he whispered, "I can't forgive Chester for hurting me. I didn't do anything to him and he just walked up and hit me. How can I forgive him?"

Max started thinking. He remembered all the things that he had done that would hurt the Lord Jesus. Then he remembered that God had forgiven everything as if it had never happened. At last, Max understood. "God, You want me to forgive Chester because You forgave me. Now I get it!"

Max sat right up in bed and said out loud, "Thank You, Lord Jesus, for helping me to understand and forgive Chester." When he was done praying, he flopped back down in bed and went right to sleep.

Day 19   Read Ephesians 4:31

Hide and Seek Words ☐
As you read your Bible try to find these hidden words:

"Let all... anger, and clamor, [noisy demands]... be put away"

Control Yourself

Max's stomach got tense and hard as he watched Chester walk toward him. "Well, if it isn't the little guy with the black eye," taunted Chester. "Hey, everybody, look at that shiner!"

Max tried to swallow the lump in his throat and he whispered, "Help me, God!"

"Boy, I bet you'd really like to get even with me, huh, Shorty," sneered Chester.

"Not anymore," said Max in a funny voice. "I'm not mad at you now."

"You're not?" said the surprised Chester. "How come?"

"Cause," explained Max, "I asked God to take the anger away from me and He did."

Chester looked at Max to see if he was teasing and then quickly walked away.

Day 20   Read Colossians 4:5

Hide and Seek Words ☐

As you read your Bible try to find these hidden words:

"Walk in wisdom"

Try to Understand

"What am I going to do about Chester, God?" prayed Max. "He doesn't go to church or believe in You. He's very bad and picks on everyone in school. Please, help me know what to do."

In the next few days, Max tried to learn everything he could about Chester. He found that Chester lived in an old house quite far from school. His father didn't live at home and his mother worked in town. Chester's big sister watched him and his brothers while his mother was away. Chester had been kept back a grade in school because he was sick and had missed so many classes. Slowly, Max began to understand. *No wonder,* thought Max. *He's older and bigger than we are and he thinks we don't like him 'cause he's different, so he's mean to us.*

Day 21   Read Philippians 2:3

Hide and Seek Words ☐
As you read your Bible try to find these hidden words:

"... let each esteem [think of the] other better than themselves"

He Is Better

"Max," said Mindy as she sat down beside him on the porch. "How is everything going with Chester?"

"Oh, all right," replied Max. "I've found out a lot about him and I understand more why he acts so bad. I'm just not sure how I should treat him."

"I know," said Mindy softly, "God says in His Word that we're to think of other people as if they are better than we are."

"Whew!" whistled Max. "That's going to be hard to do."

"Impossible," replied Mindy, "without God's help!"

"God," prayed Max, "it says in Your Word that I'm supposed to think that Chester is better than I am. I'm too selfish to do that without Your help. Please help me to obey You."

"Me, too," whispered Mindy.

Day 22   Read Titus 3:2

Hide and Seek Words □

As you read your Bible try to find these hidden words:

"...speak evil of no man"

Don't Talk Against Him

"Max!" called a boy from his class. "Come over here and tell the guys what Chester did to you yesterday."

"Aw, he's not so bad," said Max.

"Not bad?" chuckled one of the boys. "He gave you a black eye! You should be mad."

"No, not anymore," said Max.

"Say, I've been doing some checking and Chester hasn't joined any of the sport teams this year."

"He should," said one of the boys. "He's big and would play better than any of us."

He's big 'cause he's dumb and flunked out a grade," sneered another boy.

Max spoke quickly, "He stayed back a year because he was sick. I bet he feels left out because he's different from us."

"Maybe you're right," said one boy.

"Why not get him on our football team?" asked Max.

Day 23 Read 1 Peter 2:17

Hide and Seek Words ☐
As you read your Bible try to find these hidden words:

"Honor all men"

Respect Him

Chester waited until Max walked past and then ran to catch up with him. "Hi, ya, Max," he said.

Max turned and grinned at Chester. "Hi, yourself. How are you doing?" he asked.

"Okay," said Chester shyly. "I just heard that you want me to play on your football team; how come?"

"Simple," explained Max. "You know more and play better football than any of us in gym class; and we need the best for our team."

"I just can't figure you out," murmured Chester. "I've been mean to you and you're nice back to me."

"That's because I like you," said Max.

"I think you mean that," said Chester. "Would you like to be friends?" he asked.

"I sure would!" answered Max.

"That's great!" grinned Chester.

That's the first time I've ever seen him smile, thought Max. *Thank You, Lord Jesus.*

Day 24   Read 1 Timothy 6:10

Hide and Seek Words ☐

As you read your Bible try to find these hidden words:

"... the love of money is the root of all evil"

Beginning of Evil

"Max!" called Chester as he ran up the school steps. "I've got good news for you! How would you like to make a pile of money?"

"Sure," said Max uncertainly. "Who wouldn't?"

Chester's eyes glowed with hate. "We'll show those guys in our class who think they're better than we are," he hissed.

"Hold on," said Max. "I've got no argument with anybody."

"No, I guess you don't," said Chester. "But you'd like to make some money, wouldn't you?"

"Well," said Max uneasily, "that depends how we get it."

"Trust me!" bragged Chester. "I'll get us more money than you ever dreamed of."

Max felt strange inside as he listened to Chester. That night when he got ready for bed he prayed to the Lord Jesus to help him know the right thing to do—and to DO it!

Day 25   Read 1 Peter 2:13

Hide and Seek Words ☐
As you read your Bible try to find these hidden words:
"Submit yourselves to EVERY ordinance [law] of man"

Obey the Law

"Chester," asked Max softly, "exactly how are we going to make all this money?"

"Easy," Chester assured him. "I've got a brother in high school who gets some stuff from another guy to sell to the kids at school. He's been after me to sell it too. I didn't think anyone would buy from me; but they would from you, Max."

Max asked, "What kind of stuff? It isn't against the law, is it?"

"Kind of," admitted Chester. "But everyone does it now days. Nobody obeys ALL the laws anymore."

"But that's wrong!" burst out Max. "God's Word says we're supposed to obey EVERY law of man. I couldn't do anything that would break a law. I'm sorry, Chester. I don't even want to know what it is. Count me out!"

Day 26											Read James 4:17

Hide and Seek Words
As you read your Bible try to find these hidden words:
"...it is sin"

Obey Your Laws

"Boy, you're a strange one, Max," said Chester as the boys stood side by side in the school hallway. "If you're afraid to break a little law, we'll have to work out something else. Why don't you just tell the guys about the stuff I've got and let them know I'll sell it to them?"

"No!" yelled Max. "Don't you understand, Chester? I want no part of it. It's wrong!"

"You won't be breaking any law," insisted Chester.

"Yes, I would," said Max miserably. "No matter WHAT I do, if I think it's wrong, then for me it's wrong."

"But it's not against the law just to tell them to come to me," said Chester.

"It is for me," replied Max. "I would be breaking God's law, because I know I shouldn't do it."

"Okay, Pal," said the disappointed Chester. "Let me know if you change your mind."

Day 27   Read James 4:7

Hide and Seek Words ☐

As you read your Bible try to find these hidden words:

"Resist [fight] the devil"

Fight Satan

Max tossed and turned on his bed as his thoughts went thundering through his head. *MONEY...MONEY...To buy anything I want.* He couldn't stop thinking about it. "But it's wrong!" he said out loud in the darkness. Faster and faster his thoughts whirled as he thought of all the things he had ever wanted to buy.

"What's the matter with me?" he sobbed into his pillow. "I know this is wrong but I can't stop it." Suddenly, he knew what to do. He sat up in bed and said as loud as he could. "SATAN GET AWAY FROM ME! God does not want me to think this way and with His help I won't."

The whirling thoughts stopped and a calm came over Max. He felt peaceful as he got out of bed and onto his knees. With bowed head, he prayed, "Thank You, God, for showing me what to do."

Day 28   Read 2 Timothy 2:22

Hide and Seek Words □
As you read your Bible try to find these hidden words:

**"Flee [run away from]
... youthful lusts [evil desires]"**

Run from Evil

"Come here, Max, I want to show you something," called Chester. "It's right over here in my big brother's new car."

Chester ran to the back of the school parking lot and tapped on the door of a bright red car. "Hey, it's me," he called softly. Max could see the tops of the heads of some high school boys as they were slouched down in the car seats. Suddenly, the door swung open and one of the boys grabbed him.

Max looked into the blurry eyes of the boy who was holding him and he knew something was very wrong. Terrified, he jerked away and ran as fast as he could back across the school yard. "Help me, God," he prayed as his legs flew and his breath came in huge gulps. "Help me!"

Day 29   Read James 4:10

Hide and Seek Words ☐
As you read your Bible try to find these hidden words:

"... he shall lift you up"

Tell It to God

Max dropped down on the grass. "Oh, God! I've failed," he sobbed. "I thought I was doing what You wanted, but everything has gone wrong. Please, help me! "God, I really felt that You wanted me to be friends with Chester. I still think that's right. I guess I goofed when I thought about all that money. I wanted it and Chester knew it. He must think I'm a fake. I never thought I'd get mixed up in anything wrong. It happened so fast. I didn't even know what was going on. God, forgive me and somehow make this whole mess right!"

After a long time Max felt peaceful and he got up and walked home. Chester watched him as he left. He could hardly believe what he had heard. He thought, *Max believes in God. He really does.*

Day 30   Read 1 Peter 2:12

Hide and Seek Words ☐
As you read your Bible try to find these hidden words:

"... they may by your good works ... glorify God"

Others See God Through You

"Max," said Chester, "I didn't think you meant all those things you said about God, but I heard you praying yesterday. Max, does God listen to you? Does He care about you?"

"Yes," answered Max. "He cares so much that He came to earth as a man many years ago to die on the cross for our sins. He lives right now in Heaven; and He is waiting to take me there with Him after my job on earth is done. The only thing I had to do was to believe Him, tell Him the wrong things I've done, and ask Him to take them away. I'm nobody special, Chester, but God loves me and listens to me and helps me every day."

Max asked softly, "Do you know God like that?"

Chester answered, "No, I don't. But I want to, more than having all the money in the world."

Chester prayed that very night and asked the Lord Jesus to save him from his sins—because he saw God in Max's life!

Do You Love Jesus?

Day 1   Read Isaiah 43:10, 11

Hide and Seek Words ☐

As you read your Bible try to find these hidden words:

"Ye are my witnesses"

What Is a Witness?

Tommy rushed into the house. "What's the hurry, Tommy?" asked Mother.

Tommy could scarcely talk; he was so excited. "Miss Page's house is on fire," he blurted out. "The fire is coming out one of the windows. One fireman climbed up and chopped a hole in the roof. Another one put a ladder up to the window and carried out Miss Page. She was crying! Her whole house is burning up!"

"You certainly are a good witness, Tommy!" Mother said. Father, Mother and Tommy hurried over to see what they could do to help.

Tommy was a good witness. He told all he knew about the fire. A good witness for the Lord Jesus tells what he knows about Him.

Make a list of things you know about the Lord Jesus that you could tell a friend.

Day 2   Read Mark 16:15

Hide and Seek Words ☐

As you read your Bible try to find these hidden words:

"... go ... and preach the gospel"

What Does God's Witness Tell?

- G od loves us
- and
- O ffered
- His
- S on
- the
- P romised Savior,
- so that
- E veryone who believes
- may have
- L ife everlasting.

Julie could hardly wait for Good News Club™ to begin. "Guess what happened to me this week, Miss Sally! I went to visit Mr. Blake."

"Was he glad to see you?"

"Oh, yes. He asked me why *I* wanted to visit *him*. I said because I wanted to tell him about the Lord Jesus. I read John 3:16 to him from my Bible. I told him God loved him, too. I said that I wished he would receive the Lord Jesus. He can't see very well. He wants me to bring my Bible and read to him more about Him!"

Day 3   Read John 15:26, 27

Hide and Seek Words □

As you read your Bible try to find these hidden words:

"... ye also shall bear witness"

Learning to Bear Witness

Judy loved to visit Aunt Mary's house. Aunt Mary had lots of cookies in the brown cooky jar in the kitchen, and she didn't care how much milk Judy drank. It was fun, too, to play with Skipper, the dog.

Most of all Judy liked it when Aunt Mary tucked her into her big, comfortable bed and read her stories about Jesus. Judy had never heard these stories before. Sometimes she asked Aunt Mary to tell her the same story over and over. She wanted to remember it so she could tell it to her friends at home. Aunt Mary said Judy would be a witness for Jesus if she told her friends the Bible stories.

Then Aunt Mary explained. "If we love the Lord Jesus, we will talk about Him when we tell what Jesus has done for us. It is called 'bearing witness.'"

I was lost, but Jesus found me,
Cleansed my heart from all its sin.
Now I am His very own.
And I'll live for Him alone.
Ever seeking other boys and girls to win.

Day 4   Read Acts 1:8

Hide and Seek Words □
As you read your Bible try to find these hidden words:
"...ye shall be witnesses unto me"

Start Today!

Jesus was ready to return to Heaven. He gathered His disciples about Him to talk. "You shall be My witnesses right here and throughout the whole world," He told them.

If you have received the Lord Jesus as your Savior, He expects you to tell others that He wants to be their Savior, too. You can tell your parents and brothers and sisters about Him. You can tell your friends and neighbors.

You can obey the Lord Jesus' command to witness by praying each day for children in faraway lands who don't know Him. You can give some of your own money to help teach them that God loves them. By praying and giving for missionaries you can be a witness in a land far, far away.

Decide on one way you can be a witness TODAY. Ask God to help you do it!

Day 5   Read Isaiah 6:8

Hide and Seek Words ☐

As you read your Bible try to find these hidden words:

"... send me"

Send Me!

Isaiah the prophet heard the Lord asking, "Whom shall I send, and who will go for us?"

He replied, "Here am I. Send me."

Isaiah was listening. When the Lord called him, he heard.

God still calls people. By reading the Bible and thinking about it, you can find God's call to you. He will guide your thoughts.

Dear Jesus, Help me to be faithful
In reading Your Word each day.
Help me to think about what I read;
And to understand what You say.

Help me to be ready if You should call
And ask me, "Who will go?"
I want to listen and hear Your voice
Because I love You so.

Day 6 — Read Acts 8:26-29

Hide and Seek Words ☐

As you read your Bible try to find these hidden words:

"...the Spirit said...Go near"

The Witnesses' Helper

God has sent from Heaven, a Helper for His witnesses. He is the Holy Spirit.

One day God spoke to His witness, Philip, and told him to go to the desert. God knew a man was traveling there who needed to receive the Lord Jesus and have his sins forgiven. When Philip saw the man, the Holy Spirit told Philip to go near him. The man was reading the Bible, but he did not understand it. How could Philip make him understand? He could not. But the Holy Spirit could. As Philip talked, the Holy Spirit helped the man understand that Jesus died for *him* and he believed!

Trust your Helper from Heaven when you witness.

Not by might

    Nor by power

        but by My SPIRIT, saith the Lord...

            (Zechariah 4:6)

Day 7   Read 1 Corinthians 6:19

Hide and Seek Words □
As you read your Bible try to find these hidden words:

"... ye are not your own"

All for God!

If you are God's child, He wants you to use your body for Him. To find out how, look up the verses in God's Word. Then fill in the blanks with one of these words:

EAR MOUTH HAND FEET

Ecclesiastes 9:10 "Whatsoever thy _____ findeth to do, do it with thy might...."

Romans 10:15 "...How beautiful are the _____ of them that preach the gospel of peace..."

Revelation 2:29 "He that hath an _____, let him hear..."

Psalm 89:1 "...with my _____ will I make known thy faithfulness..."

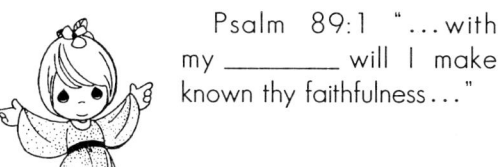

Day 8   Read Matthew 2:1, 2

Hide and Seek Words ☐
As you read your Bible try to find these hidden words:
"Where is he?"

A Star Leads the Way

Terry was sitting on the back porch with Mike, looking at the beautiful stars. One star shone brighter than the others.

"Do you see that big star, Mike?" asked Terry.

"Yeah! It's really a beauty, isn't it? I wonder why it's so much brighter than the others."

"I don't know about that one, but I know about another bright star. When the Lord Jesus was born in Bethlehem, the wise men who came looking for Him followed a bright star."

"Really? How did they know the star would lead them to a baby?"

"Their prophets wrote about it. The prophets were men God chose to tell His messages to the people. Come on. I'll get my Bible and show you."

"Will you? Let's go!" said Mike.

Many people are still wondering, "How can we find the Lord Jesus?" They need *your* help!

Day 9 Read Jonah 3:1-4

Hide and Seek Words ☐

As you read your Bible try to find these hidden words:

"...go...and preach"

Don't Be a Jonah!

God told Jonah to go to Nineveh. He was to tell the people to turn from their sins. But Jonah did not want to go. He wanted God to destroy Nineveh!

Jonah tried to run away from God. He got into a ship to go to another city. But God sent a great storm. God's Word tells us that Jonah begged the sailors to throw him into the sea so the storm would stop. The men didn't want to throw him over, but after they did, the waters became calm.

God prepared a big fish to swallow Jonah. When he was inside the fish, Jonah confessed his sin of disobeying God. Then God spoke to the fish and it spit Jonah out on the land.

Again God told Jonah to go to Nineveh. This time he went! He had learned to obey God.

Trust and obey,
For there's no other way,
To be happy in Jesus,
But to trust and obey.
—J. H. Sammis

Day 10   Read Acts 27:23-25

Hide and Seek Words ☐

As you read your Bible try to find these hidden words:

"I believe God"

Believing God

A mighty wind arose at sea. The ship on which the missionary Paul was traveling was caught in the storm. For many days the sailors did not see the sun or stars. They thought they would all be drowned.

But God told Paul that all the people on the ship would be safe. Paul told the sailors not to be afraid. He said, "Take courage. I believe God!"

Is it hard for you to be a witness for the Lord Jesus? God has promised, "Fear not, for I am with you... I will strengthen you, yes, I will help you...." (See Deuteronomy 41:10.) If you believe God will help you witness for Him, print the Hide and Seek Words here:

Day 11   Read 1 Timothy 4:12

Hide and Seek Words ☐
As you read your Bible try to find these hidden words:

"...be thou an example of the believers"

The Faithful Follower

In the blanks, write the first letter of each Bible verse below:

___ ___ ___ ___ ___ ___ ___

"Watch therefore; for ye know not what hour your Lord doth come" (Matthew 24:42). (Be ready for Jesus to return for you.)

"In all thy ways acknowledge him, and he shall direct thy paths" (Proverbs 3:6). (Put Jesus first in everything and He will guide you.)

"Trust in the Lord with all thine heart..." (Proverbs 3:5). (Never be afraid.)

"Neglect not the gift that is in thee" (1 Timothy 4:14). (Use the abilities God has given you.)

"Exalt the Lord our God" (Psalm 99:9). (Praise the Lord.)

"Serve the Lord with gladness" (Psalm 100:2).

"Sing unto the Lord" (Psalm 30:4).

A faithful follower of the Lord Jesus is a good witness. Read the verses again and <u>underline</u> an action word in each verse which tells you what you should do. (One verse tells something you should *not* do.)

Day 12   Read John 1:40-42

Hide and Seek Words ☐

As you read your Bible try to find these hidden words:

"...he brought him to Jesus"

Have You Told Your Brother?

Andrew told his brother
>he had met the Lord.

He rushed right out to tell him
>with a happy word.

He brought Peter to the Savior
>and that made him glad;

For Christ became the best Friend
>that Peter ever had.

Andrew was happy when Christ called him to follow. He just couldn't wait to tell his brother so he could know Jesus, too.

Have you told someone about the Lord Jesus? You can tell someone TODAY!

PRAYER

Dear Lord, I pray You will help me to tell others about You. I want to be a witness like Andrew. In Jesus' name. Amen

Day 13   Read John 1:43-45

Hide and Seek Words ☐

As you read your Bible try to find these hidden words:

"Philip findeth Nathanael"

Finding Our Friends

It was the day after Andrew had brought his brother Peter to the Lord. Jesus had decided to go to Galilee. There He found Philip. He said to Philip, "Come, follow me."

Philip was very happy that Jesus had called him. In fact, he was so happy he ran to find his friend Nathanael. When he found him, he said, "We have found the Messiah. His name is Jesus. Come with us to see Him!"

God's Word tells us that Philip brought Nathanael to Jesus. Like Philip, Nathanael became one of Jesus' twelve disciples. He was called Bartholomew. How happy he was that his friend had brought him to Jesus.

Have *you* told *your* friends about the Lord Jesus?

PRAYER

Dear Lord Jesus, please help me today to tell my friends about You. Amen

Day 14   Read Acts 2:32

Hide and Seek Words ☐
As you read your Bible try to find these hidden words:

"... we all are witnesses"

Witnessing to Friends

Megan opened her eyes. She yawned sleepily. Then she remembered it was Sunday. She jumped out of bed and ran down the hall. "Wake up! Wake up, Jamie!" She shouted. "Today Sam and Patti are going with us to Sunday school."

The past Sunday Miss Gray had told the children the Lord Jesus wanted them to tell others about His love for them. "Bring your friends with you to Sunday school," she told them. "We can study about the Lord Jesus together."

Megan and Jamie had invited Sam and Patti. They were happy that their neighbors had agreed to go.

"Maybe today they will receive Jesus as their Savior," Jamie said happily.

Before they left Megan prayed. "Dear Jesus, we thank You that Sam and Patti are coming with us. Please help us to be good witnesses to them. We pray that they will receive You as their Savior, too. Amen."

Day 15 — Read Matthew 18:14

Hide and Seek Words ☐
As you read your Bible try to find these hidden words:
"...not...one...should perish"

Winning a Friend

Carrie loved the Lord Jesus. She wished her friend Kim would receive Him. *Maybe Kim doesn't know who Jesus is,* she thought. *I am going to pray for her.*

Carrie closed her eyes. "Dear Jesus, Kim needs You as her Savior. Help her to see that You died for her sins, too."

Carrie prayed for Kim every day. She was glad they were attending vacation Bible school together. As they walked home, they talked about their Bible stories. Carrie told Kim about the time she had received the Lord Jesus.

On the last day of vacation Bible school Carrie asked, "Kim, don't you want to receive the Lord Jesus?"

Kim looked surprised. A smile spread across her face. "I already have," she replied. "When you told me what Jesus had done for you, I asked Him to be my Savior from sin, too!"

If you think Carrie thanked God, you are right!

Day 16　　　　　　　　Read Deuteronomy 6:12

Hide and Seek Words □
As you read your Bible try to find these hidden words:

"...beware lest thou forget the Lord"

Helping Our Christian Friends

Erin and Heather had received the Lord Jesus as their Savior on the same day. It was fun learning new things from God's Word together. Then Heather moved away.

Erin and Carla became pals after that. Carla did not know the Lord Jesus as her Savior. Erin began to forget her promises to put the Lord Jesus first. Some days she never thought of Him.

One day Heather came to visit. As she was getting ready for bed, she said to Erin, "Let's read our Bibles together." Erin didn't even know where her Bible was!

"Oh, Erin, are you forgetting about Jesus? He loved us so much He died for us!"

Erin looked down. "I'm glad you came to visit, Heather. I was forgetting. Will He forgive me?"

"I know He will! Let's ask Him."

"Dear Jesus," Erin prayed, "I'm sorry I haven't been putting you first in my life. Please forgive me."

Day 17   Read Galatians 6:9, 10

Hide and Seek Words ☐

As you read your Bible try to find these hidden words:

"... let us do good unto all men"

Helping the Helpless

When she was a young girl, Mrs. Hess had received the Lord Jesus as her Savior. Now she is old and spends all her time in a wheelchair. But she is not discouraged. When Sunday comes, she is always at church.

How do you think Mrs. Hess gets to church in a wheelchair? Her neighbors take her there every week. They remind me of the four men in the Bible who brought a sick man to Jesus.

PRAYER

Dear Jesus, please help me to be very kind to sick people. Help me to show them how much You love them.

Day 18   Read Acts 16:23-25

Hide and Seek Words ☐
As you read your Bible try to find these hidden words:

"... **prayed, and sang praises**"

Don't Get Discouraged!

Would you thank God if you were put into prison for telling others about the Lord Jesus? Paul and Silas did! They sang and prayed while they were in prison. The other prisoners listened.

Then there was an earthquake! The prison doors were opened and the jailer thought his prisoners would escape. When Paul and Silas didn't try to get away, the jailer asked, "What must I do to be saved?" Paul and Silas answered, "Believe on the Lord Jesus Christ...." The jailer believed and his life was changed!

Paul and Silas were faithful witnesses even in prison. They weren't discouraged. Don't let God's enemy, Satan, discourage you from talking and singing about the Lord Jesus.

Day 19   Read Psalm 119:172

Hide and Seek Words

As you read your Bible try to find these hidden words:

"My tongue shall speak of thy word"

God's Workers

Look up these verses and see who God's speakers were. Then fill in the puzzle.

1) Acts 17:22
2) Acts 10:34
3) Jonah 3:4
4) Exodus 4:30

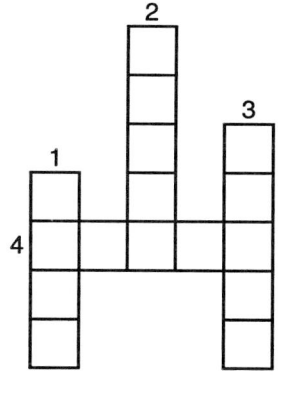

God used _____ to tell of His love. He will use you if you will let Him.

Answers to puzzle on Day 30.

Day 20   Read John 9:4

Hide and Seek Words ☐

As you read your Bible try to find these hidden words:

"... night cometh, when no man can work"

Doing Our Father's Will

Mark raked the leaves quickly. He wanted to finish before dark. His dad had promised to take him hiking if he got his work done. As he piled the leaves into the basket, Mark thought about what his Bible club teacher had said.

"Each boy and girl must do the work God assigns him. Jesus did the work of His Heavenly Father. We should do the work of our Heavenly Father, also. This work is to tell people about the Lord Jesus."

Mark scooped up the last pile of leaves as the first star began to twinkle. Now he understood what his teacher meant. Just as he needed to rake the leaves before his dad returned, he needed to tell others about the Lord Jesus before He returned to take him to Heaven. Read your Hide and Seek Words again.

PRAYER

Dear Jesus, help me to be busy working for You.

Day 21　　　　　　　　　　Read 2 Corinthians 9:7

Hide and Seek Words ☐
As you read your Bible try to find these hidden words:
"God loveth a cheerful giver"

God's Tomatoes

Pam and Micah sat by the roadside. Above their heads a sign read, "GARDEN FRESH TOMATOES." Father said the children could keep the money they earned selling tomatoes. They decided to give it all to their missionary friends.

Soon a shiny blue car pulled up. "How much are your tomatoes, children?"

"Fifty cents a basket. They were picked today!"

"I'd like two baskets, please," said the lady.

Pam thanked her for the dollar. Micah put the tomatoes into the car. By the end of the day they had $8 to send to the missionaries, and a special happiness in their hearts!

> It's time to give, it's time to give
> That other boys and girls may live...
> With Jesus in their hearts each day.
> I want to give; this is God's way.

Day 22   Read John 6:13

Hide and Seek Words ☐
As you read your Bible try to find these hidden words:
"There is a lad here"

Giving What We Have

One day a boy gave the Lord Jesus his lunch. Jesus used the lunch to feed 5,000 men. When the men had finished eating, there were twelve baskets full of food left. Jesus had done a great miracle. The boy was happy that he had given his lunch.

The Lord Jesus is pleased to use boys and girls in His work today. You can give what you have to Jesus. You can give part of your money in the offerings at Good News Club. You can pass out tracts that tell about the Lord Jesus. You can invite others to go with you to club or Sunday school.

When you do this, you are allowing the Lord to use what you have. You are like the lad who gave his lunch.

Day 23   Read 2 Thessalonians 3:1

Hide and Seek Words ☐

As you read your Bible try to find these hidden words:

"...pray for us"

Serving God Now

Ben's mother tucked him into bed and went to her room. She was nearly asleep when she heard sobs. Quietly she went to Ben's room.

"Ben, are you sick?" she asked.

Tears were running down Ben's cheeks. "Oh, Mother," he sobbed, "I was thinking about all the boys and girls who don't know about the Lord Jesus. I want to go and tell them so they can receive Him."

Mother quietly explained that God would help him tell other boys and girls.

"But what can I do right now?" Ben wondered.

"You can pray for one of our missionary friends. Why don't you pray for the missionary who visited our church and has gone back to Africa?" asked Mother.

"I can do that. I'll pray for him right now," Ben said as he kneeled by his bed. He prayed, too, for friends he would meet the next day who still did not know the Lord Jesus. "Good night, Mother," he said as he crawled back in bed.

Day 24   Read Matthew 10:19, 20

Hide and Seek Words □
As you read your Bible try to find these hidden words:

"It shall be given you"

Troy Invites His Teacher

Ringgggggggggggggg! It was the closing bell. The children hurried to catch their buses. All the children but Troy. His mother was picking him up later.

Troy got his jacket and hurried down the hall. Outside Mr. Greene's door he stopped. He bowed his head. "Please, God," he prayed, "help me know what to say." He knocked lightly.

"Come in!" said Troy's favorite teacher.

"Hi, Mr. Greene. May I talk with you a minute?"

"Of course, Troy. What's the problem?"

"No problem, Mr. Greene, I wanted to invite you to our church services on Sunday."

"Why that's very kind of you. I would like to visit your church. Thank you for asking me. What time does the service begin?"

After Troy answered he prayed in his heart, "Thank You, Lord Jesus, for helping me speak for you!"

Day 25   Read Acts 4:18-20

Hide and Seek Words ☐

As you read your Bible try to find these hidden words:

"... we cannot but speak"

We Can't Keep Quiet!

God had given Peter and John power to heal a lame man. Now the chief priests were angry with them. They told Peter and John they must never speak about Jesus again. Peter and John replied in words which meant, "We can't stop telling about the wonderful things we saw the Lord Jesus do and heard Him say."

The authorities threatened Peter and John. Then they let them go. Many people praised God for the wonderful miracle of healing the lame man.

Peter and John kept on telling about Jesus because they knew God wanted them to.

STOP and let me tell you what the Lord has done for me!

Day 26 Read 1 Peter 3:15

Hide and Seek Words
As you read your Bible try to find these hidden words:

"**. . . be ready always to give an answer**"

Ready to Answer

Pete's folks were planning a picnic for Sunday and invited Josh to go along. They wanted to leave right after breakfast so they could get to the beach early. Josh liked picnics, but he didn't want to miss Sunday school.

Since the day he had received the Lord Jesus, Josh had not missed Sunday school once. He liked learning about Jesus.

"Surely you can miss one Sunday!" said Pete.

"But, Pete," Josh explained, "when I asked the Lord Jesus to come into my heart, I promised to be faithful to Him. The Bible says we should meet together with others who love the Lord Jesus."

Pete thought for a moment. "I'll talk to Dad. Maybe we can have our picnic in the park after you get home from Sunday school. Jesus must be pretty important to you if you would miss a picnic to go to Sunday school. I'd like to hear more about Him."

Day 27   Read 1 John 1:3, 4

Hide and Seek Words □

As you read your Bible try to find these hidden words:

"**. . . these things write we unto you**"

Witnessing with a Letter

Sherry wrote a letter to her friend. She brought the envelope to her mother. "Mommy, will you write Sandy's address for me?"

"Surely," said Mother. "I'm glad you wrote Sandy. Her mom and dad don't know the Lord Jesus as their Savior. But Sandy loves Him very much.

"Mommy, what could I do to help Sandy's mommy and daddy?"

Mother thought a moment. "You know those little papers we have that tell about God's love for people?"

"You call them tracts, don't you?" Sherry asked.

"Yes, let's choose one to send to Sandy's folks."

Before they put the tract into the envelope they prayed that Sandy's parents would learn to love the Lord Jesus, too.

Day 28   Read Acts 20:20, 21

Hide and Seek Words ☐

As you read your Bible try to find these hidden words:

"I ... have taught you ... from house to house"

Telling from House to House

Gary was happy as he ran home from Sunday school. Miss Phillips had given a surprise announcement to the boys and girls. "Tuesday afternoon we are beginning a Bible story hour. We will have it once a week. You may invite your friends to come with you," she said.

Gary had some new neighbors. Three families had moved in right after school ended. There were lots of kids he could invite! Gary would be like Jesus' follower, Paul. He would go from house to house, telling the boys and girls about Jesus and inviting them to the story hour. How excited he was!

    Ringing doorbells, ringing doorbells,
    Ringing doorbells for my Lord.
    Wearing out my shoes,
    Telling God's good news,
    Ringing doorbells for my Lord.

Day 29   Read Mark 16:5-8

Hide and Seek Words ☐
As you read your Bible try to find these hidden words:

"And they went out quickly"

Hurry! Hurry!

Mary and some other women came to the place where Jesus' body had been buried. When they arrived, they saw an angel. They were surprised! The angel said, "Fear not. I know you are looking for Jesus. He is not here. He is risen. Go quickly and tell His disciples."

God's Word says that the women went out quickly. They ran to tell everyone that Jesus was alive again.

Many boys and girls believe in gods who are dead or who are made out of wood and stone. It is exciting to know that the Lord Jesus is alive! Can you go quickly and tell this good news to someone who doesn't know?

Jesus
Go tell He is risen,
Go tell He can save;
Go tell He can meet ev'ry need;
Go tell He arose from the grave.*

*Copyright © 1972, by Sacred Music Foundation.
All rights reserved.

Day 30   Read Joshua 1:8, 9

Hide and Seek Words ☐

As you read your Bible try to find these hidden words:

"...the Lord...is with thee"

Get Ready, Get Set, Go!

Joshua obeyed God as a young man. God knew Joshua could be trusted to be the leader of His people. In your Bible verses for today, you will find some rules that God gave to Joshua. They are rules that can help you be a good witness.

Speak God's Word.
Think about (meditate on) God's Word.
Obey God's Word.
Don't be afraid.
Remember, God is with you wherever you go.

Answers to puzzle for Day 19

		P		
		E		
		T		J
	P	E		O
A	A	R	O	N
	U			A
	L			H

(2-Down: PETER; 1-Down: PAUL; 3-Down: JONAH; 4-Across: AARON)